# THOSE KIDS

## are OUR kids

Heidy LaFleur

# Heidy with a WHY, Inc.

# Mission

Equip administrators, teachers and all educators with **practical** strategies to make all kids feel successful; especially those who've been traumatized, are misunderstood and those who practice frequent detours from what's expected.

ISBN: 9798671740400

# Testimonials

*In today's world our children are faced with many challenges that sometimes we are not aware of or prepared to handle. Heidy's message is POWERFUL! Her experiences as an educator and a parent need to be heard by everyone that either has a child or works with children. Heidy is very passionate about helping every adult understand that we can not fix children but we can definitely help them along the way. Her story is real and it has helped adults understand why children may act the way they do. Heidy provides you with tools that help build trust and allow you to understand the needs of the children in your life. She is one of my favorite speakers that I have listened to and her story and creative way of engaging her audience empowers them to want to help EVERY child!*

**-Dr. Shwkar Abousweilem, 2019 IPA South Cook Elementary Principal of the Year, Principal, Burbank School, Burbank, Illinois**

*Today we are facing uncertain times and Heidy's book, Those Kids are OUR Kids is the call to action we need. Her passionate story-telling, her inspiring words, and her dedication to the success of all students is a message we need to keep sharing with educators and communities around the globe. From personal experiences to challenging truths, every page of this book allows the reader to reflect, seek to understand, grow, and lead conversations with those around them in the HOPE of creating positive transformations. Her creativity, her voice, and her unwavering support of trauma-informed practice are quintessential elements for all leadership teams and school families. I am grateful for her courage and strength in sharing words of encouragement.*

**-Roman Nowak, Teacher/Student Success Leader/Agent of Transformation - Rockland, Ontario, Canada**

*Certain people come into your life with purpose and understanding. Heidy LaFleur always had the understanding of "Those Kids." This true story takes you on a personal journey of trauma to explain how all those years of understanding her students helped her survive. She is a natural leader that gets "it". Every educator needs this book at the ready. You will not look at any child the same way after reading Those Kids are OUR Kids. "Those kids" frustrate us, confuse us, and emotionally drain us. But what Heidy will teach you is that when you make the connection that child needs you will never forget "that kid" and that child will never forget the time you took to understand.*
  **-Theresa Hehn, MEd. Curriculum & Instruction, NBCT Adolescence Science, Chicago Public Schools**

*From the introduction, Heidy draws you in to the why you must read this book. As I read the book, I reimagine my purpose and vision as the principal of an inner-city school where many of our students have experienced some form of trauma. If you are looking for a book that will help you and your staff move from thinking "these kids" can't to "those kids" can, this book is a must read. Those Kids sparks hope and compassion back in the hearts of all as you read and experience the pain and triumphs through Heidy's personal stories. If you only have one book that you can incorporate and embed into your school culture, Those Kids is it.*
  **-Mrs. Fabian Daniels, Proud Principal, Harrison Community Learning Center, Peoria, Illinois**

*I have been in education for 48 years and Heidy is one of the most dynamic and inspirational speakers that I have ever heard. Y'all have a treasure in her.*
  **-Ruth Meche, Principal, St. Christopher School, New Orleans, Louisiana**

*Heidy Pemsl LaFleur's book, "Those Kids are OUR Kids" really hits home. All kids must matter. Their life has a sto-*

*ry we all need to understand and give time to. This book is a powerful reminder of what can happen in times of neglect, panic, and being labeled. This is a book for not only educators, but parents and community members to read, understand and experience. There are so many stories, anecdotes, and problem solving perspectives in this book, that it is a must have. Some choices and patterns that have remained in education, "just because", but are so detrimental to our students MUST be looked at, discussed and changed. Heidy brings up topics that must not be ignored. Thank you for this powerful, emotional and eye opening book that will help us remember to look at each child as an individual, and figure out a way to support them, now.*
**-Jeff Kubiak, Educator, Author of "One Drop of Kindness", and "It's Me", Speaker and advocate for inclusion and equity in education.**

*Heidy LaFleur is a caring visionary who speaks truth in a time of need. Her book "Those kids are OUR kids" is an all-encompassing book that details every kids' worth. At a time when we need it most, Heidy comes through with a book that gives you the tools to handle any situation. Her vulnerability in telling her personal story will forever endear you to her. Do not let another day go by without getting this book and the 26 strategies that will make you a better teacher, principal, and person. Heidy was a successful long-time principal who uses her failures and successes to tell her story. A genuine person who connects real life experiences to the situations we go through on a daily basis. Her books always resonate with educators and are necessary reads for any educator. She is a real breath of fresh air in the education world. I know you will enjoy getting to know her better through her books and keynote speeches.*
**-Joe R. Toomey, President, Alabama Association of Secondary Principals, 2020 Dr. Martin Luther King, Jr. Drum Major Award, 2015 National Blue Ribbon School Principal, National Speaker**

*Great leadership is established in the opportunity to show up courageously for the communities you serve. In both my work with Heidy and by witnessing her story, I observed just that: a brave educator who is fueled by her*

*power to overcome significant obstacles in parenting as well as teaching and learning through it all. She's taken these powerful lessons on human relationships - to be who she needed during hard times (and still needs)- to establish an accessible, universal language we can all use while growing our skill set to better serve students and families.*
**-Claire Oliver, Ed S., NCSP, Nationally Certified School Psychologist**

*After reading this book, all I can say is POWERFUL! Every single person in education should be required to read this. This is eye-opening and heartbreaking. Empower over Ego is a must, along with Compassion over Curriculum! I loved the solutions and ideas. Even as a teacher going into my 15th year of teaching, I had to reflect on situations and how things were handled. I hope this reaches as many hands as possible!*
**-Krista Davidson, Second Grade Teacher, Colorado**

*A Must Read for ANY educator! "Those Kids" is an authentic and heartfelt experience into the true impact of trauma and the courage and tenacity that one family used to stand strong and do what is undeniably best for all students. Those Kids is a truly unique blend of raw emotion paired with simple steps educators can take to ensure that all children are given a voice. This book will leave every educator with feelings of encouragement and influence to ensure that connection is the foundation of our journey with students and to empower educators to see students for who they truly are instead of who we may want them to be. Reading along I was captivated by the author's undeniable ability to share the pain and uncertainty while also sharing hope for all students for our future. Those kids truly are OUR kids!*
**-Lindsay Titus, M.Ed, BCBA, DEFINE YOUniversity Founder**

*Thank you Heidy LaFleur for being transparent and writing about your personal experience dealing with trauma as a mother, educator, and wife. The canoe illustration at the beginning and relating it to parenting is fantastic. Your*

*vulnerability and willingness to give insight into your families' pain and triumph, so that others can get free is refreshing. This resource causes me to re-evaluate how I lead, how I parent, how I teach, and how I train, and work with my own children, students, and adults. Heidy has produced a resource not limited to those serving in education; furthermore it is for adults that are raising and rearing children. This resource provides parenting leadership tools and the framework for resolving conflict through a healthy, balanced and transparent approach.* **A MUST READ.**
>       **-H. Goode, President of Goode Solutions, Author,**
>       **Speaker, Radio Talk Show Host, Father, Husband**

*Being able to meet and hear Heidy Pemsl LaFleur speak in person had such a tremendous impact on our school district. With the school year coming to an end and in the middle of the Covid-19 pandemic, our staff still referenced Heidy's words from last fall. Being able to have "Those Kids" in our hands is exciting! Think of all of the departments that will benefit from reading this and having small group discussions; counselors, teachers, associates, bus drivers, etc. Thank you for sharing your story and giving us the gift of what does work for all kids, especially those kids!*
>       **-Kristin C. Hicks, Associate Director of Student Services,**
>       **Linn-Mar Community School District**

*Heidy writes from the heart. She combines years of educational experience and traumatic events her family has endured to give a first hand account of students' behaviors from the other side. An eye opening book that provides educators and parents alike a guide on easy implementable steps and strategies to better reach and understand ALL kids. A powerful book that shows how a slight change in delivery could have a lasting impact on a child's life. It is evident that Heidy is a fighter and someone who cares deeply about children.*
>       **-Charlie Curtin, National Board Certified Special Education Teacher, Illinois**

*Heidy LaFleur shares her heartfelt vision for creating a culture of caring in schools that is rooted in her own struggles as a parent, administrator and advocate. Now more than ever for the sustainability of our quality of life, and accessibility to life long learning, her perspective is a needed and welcome voice of reason rooted in experience and a commitment to using her own adversities to help others. Her story of advocating for her son is a comfort to parents struggling to navigate a sometimes confusing and rigid system. Her administrator insight can stretch the perspective of those in the educational trenches.*
**-Alison Redding, Special Education Director, Chicago, Illinois**

*Heidy continues to make it her life's work to help the students who really need it. She has been a teacher, administrator, a professional development speaker, and now she speaks from her soul in her book. Heidy has combined her years in education and as a mother to create this one of a kind resource. Heidy has made a tool that allows all of us to help each child in our classrooms and schools. Applying these strategies will help change the lives of those kids!*
**-Elisabeth Betancourt, School Social Worker**

*In a very honest and raw account of her son's struggle with PTSD and depression, Heidy self-discloses the struggles she had with her son as he experienced one of the worst situations that a mother fears that her child will go through. The hardship her marriage, family and relationships took was heart-wrenching as she tried to help her son and get the care he deserved. From counselors, to teachers, to administrators, Heidy reached out to plead for help for her child. Having been an educator she knew what protocol was to be followed and oh the frustration she felt because the system had lost itself and its purpose- To help "Those Kids" feel safe, secure and that they matter.*

*This book is an eye-opening story, one that is true to the heart, but one that will open the eyes of many educators. It brings us back to the "why" - why did we become educators. Many of us will say to make a difference in this world. It is now your turn. Make a difference in this world. Read her story. Feel it and hear it. Then continue to read. Heidy has taken effective traits and strategies and created alliterations that explain how educators, teachers and parents can successfully work with children who have gone through trauma.*

*Pay close attention to each alliteration and take time to reflect. Then remember. Remember that the child sitting in your class may be silently crying out for help. Learn their story, listen to them with an open heart. Know that you can be the difference in that child's life. After all, as Heidy states, relationships are what will help a child flourish. This book will be a tool you use whether you are just beginning your career as a teacher or as a 30-year veteran. Open the book. Begin to read it because "Those Kids"are worth it. They need us.*

**-Brenda Jones, M.Ed., Franklin B. Walter Award Recipient, Kindergarten Teacher, Avon Lake, OH**

To my husband, Garrett for walking this journey with me, believing in me & loving me through it. We make an awesome team.

To Lilly, my beautiful oldest and only daughter. You are such an old soul and this world will always benefit from your kindness, love, work ethic and compassion for what's right.

To G, my talented artist and vocalist middle child. The world will never define you. You will define you and you are the key to your happiness.

To Peter, who will always be my baby. Sporty, funny and so grown up in a young body. Your goodness and humor shine in all you do.

I love all of you always and forever.

# Table of Contents

# Preface

This book shares my story as a mother of a child who was sexually abused in a public school. There may be parts of this story that make you uncomfortable and for that I apologize. In order to learn and grow, I believe that sometimes we have to be moved, shocked and uncomfortable. I share this preface with you because I want to be sensitive to those who've been through trauma and understand the heart ache and constant reclaiming of life that it brings. This story comes from deep in my heart and I share it for two reasons. First, because it could have been prevented and I never want another family to suffer as we have. Second, the strategies and stories I share can help all educators understand the power of human connection that our kids crave & will open many eyes to pay close attention to the reason behind behavior.

That said, I present to you practical strategies to work with kids who've been traumatized, misunderstood and those who take frequent detours from what's expected. The following suggestions come from years of experience working with my son, and over 20 years experience working with kids that so badly want to be loved and accepted by adults. Those who are helped and understood by the adults around them, heal, and reclaim life with time. Kids who don't get the attention they need and crave, get defiant. They are the really misunderstood ones. They are "Those Kids."

Know that some refer to "Those Kids" as the needy, annoying, disrespectful ones who take up a lot of our time. The reality is "Those

Kids" are OUR Kids and my goal is to teach you how to build relationships with all kids so all kids can thrive. Often educators are not taught how to work with trauma, mental illness, special needs and kids who don't sit and listen to us. I want to share my understanding of trauma, the importance of your Actions, Words & Expressions (AWE) and how to build a foundation of relationships before all else.

We are all flawed. We need to focus on excellence, not perfection. We need to be better next year than last year. Better next month than this month and better tomorrow than today.
-Adolph Brown

# Becoming one of "Those Kids"

I t was a cold winter night ingrained in my memory forever. My husband was at the firehouse as he was every third day. After a long day, my three kids and I were getting ready for bed. Our world blew up in a matter of minutes and we have worked tirelessly to reclaim our son, our family, our marriage and myself ever since. Just after 8:00 PM on February 7, 2012 my six-year-old son came out of the bathroom and started to cry like I had never heard before. The feel was different. The look in his eyes was different. The thumping in my chest, different. He clung to my thigh and said, "Mom please love me. Please love me. I didn't know. I am so sorry. I didn't know. Please love me." As I held my three-year-old, and my seven-year-old looked on, the words were like a slow blur coming from his mouth that punched me square in the face.

As he continued to cry, he spoke through tears and fright. "Mom it happened in the bathroom. Please still love me. I didn't know." He sobbed and sobbed and held my leg. He told me what happened to him in the bathroom during recess. I was completely numb and felt sick to my stomach. He got extremely quiet and would only talk in short, sorrowful whispers for the next five months. He didn't sleep which meant I didn't sleep. He acted out. He threw things. He swore. He yelled and screamed and cried. He was despondent and grieving and somber. He didn't want to go to school anymore. My other children didn't understand why their brother was "acting like that." My husband didn't understand why he was becoming disobedient & disrespectful and I started losing my best friend because we saw things from differing parenting perspectives.

I reported my son's words to the administration at his school and didn't receive a call back from the principal for 10 days. His voicemail apologized for the "mishap." I spoke with the assistant principal and told her what my son said and who the child was in the bathroom with him. She shared that she wasn't surprised because the kid acted like the kids she dealt with at one of the foster homes in Chicago. At the time, I didn't understand what she meant because I didn't know much about traumatized kids. Later the same day, I got a call from the school counselor telling me that I needed to get my son into counseling immediately because according to her interviews with teachers & kids the abuse started in May of kindergarten and ended in October of first grade.

I knew therapy was inevitable. I made an appointment for our first therapy session and after the intake, the agency asked if I wanted a number for an attorney. Hiring an attorney was something that never crossed my mind. I didn't consider us the suing type. On our way to our first therapy appointment, I called the doctor because I was terrified I wasn't doing the right thing. My son was screaming in the car and begging me to take him home. She said it was going to be a hard road ahead and to just keep driving. After she met with him alone, she called my husband and me back to her office. She said she had something very serious to share with us. She said our son was suicidal and also knew how he wanted to kill his sister. She said we needed to put the knives in our home away and watch our son twenty-four hours a day. She said he shouldn't be left alone with his siblings. Oh my God.

Each day my son would tell me a little more about what happened in the bathroom. Therapy continued three times per week. He was diagnosed with Post Traumatic Stress Disorder (PTSD) and major depressive disorder. My son then shared that there was a third kid in the bathroom with them sometimes. I called the assistant principal to let her know that there was another student involved. The counselor interviewed that student and sure enough, his stories matched my sons.

At the time, I was in the 12th year of my career. Serving as a teacher in the Chicago Public School system for eight years, I was four years into serving as an assistant principal at the same school. I was a finalist for a principal position at a different Chicago Public School, and was invited to a finalist forum on February 18th so the school community and public could see and hear the candidates and ask questions. I wasn't able to attend because my life plans took a sharp turn on the night of February 12th. After calling the Local School Council president and withdrawing my name from the list of finalists, she informed me that I was the one they wanted. I was so disappointed & discouraged. I was muddled, frightened and an emotional mess. Trying to keep it all together with my job, my marriage and three little kids, I started the search to understand what happened to my son. Just as some of our kids and families take detours in life, I was starting to create mine and I was scared to death.

I now had a son who was tormented by his mind, confused, scared and shameful. He would talk in gut wrenching whispers sharing, "Mom, I have to tell you something else that happened." Each day was a tearful and quiet soul barf of events that brought such pain to my ears and heart. The abuser told my son if he told anyone about it, he would be in big trouble. The abuser told my son he was fat and was going to hell. He asked my son why God ever made him. **My son was sexually abused by a peer in a public school bathroom for the last two months of kindergarten and the first two months of first grade.**

The more healthy relationships a child has, the more likely he will be to recover from trauma and thrive. Relationships are the agents of change and the most powerful therapy is human love.

-Dr. Bruce Perry

# Becoming one of "Those Kids" takeaways

- Trauma is an emotional response to a disturbing event.

- Repeated exposure to trauma dramatically impacts self-esteem, behavior, perception of others' intentions, appropriate peer interaction, overall understanding of the world and brain chemistry.

- Kids often feel "emotionally stuck" which leads to what may look like defiance.

- Trauma leads to internal war, which leads to misunderstood behaviors, which oftentimes leads to punishment because we don't realize that behavior is a way to articulate fear, sadness, anger and confusion.

- The trauma cycle consists of internal factors > external factors (triggers) > behaviors > human response

- Internally, kids may feel sad, desperate, lonely, frustrated, abandoned, out of control, lost, vulnerable, angry & anxious. They can also experience muscle tension, stomach aches, headaches, racing heart & nightmares.

    * They feel this way because of external factors, called triggers. A trigger can be anything associated with the trauma, anything that reminds them of the trauma or a random, fearful and unsettling thought. A few examples are, seeing the abuser, smelling a certain scent, a location, a time, a holiday, time away from school, perceived danger and bad weather.

    * With triggers, come behaviors that can look like defiance. As educators, we may see crying, hiding, running, sleepiness, lack of interest, lack of concentration, emotional outbursts, denial, act-

ing out physically, panic attacks, silence, irritability or sitting alone.

✳ The only thing we have control over is human response to behavior.

- The trauma cycle comes and goes. Kids can appear "fine" but when a trigger hits, their demeanor can change entirely for a period of time.

- Coping with a traumatic event is a life-long commitment and the adults surrounding a child can either help a child soar, or add weight to a child's already compromised state.

- Oftentimes, kids don't tell anyone about abuse because they think they will be in trouble or they did something bad.

- Trauma behavior doesn't just "go away." Trauma is not something you just get over.

- As educators, we have to work hard not to take student behavior personally. Kids who've been traumatized aren't upset with us, but sometimes, we are the outlet.

# Raising one of "Those Kids"

As my questions and search for understanding how this could possibly happen grew, so did my anxiety. I felt the most distant, uncomfortable depression overcome me. Back at my school, I was far from myself. I was the one who used to come in with a smile, and a helping heart each day. Instead, I was sad and numb and felt as if my life were out of control. So many unanswered questions and emotions I couldn't understand or explain. At home, I was living a new life. In both places, I felt like I had to pretend everything was ok and it was painful.

During after school talks with my kids, I heard this child's name often. He was a topic of conversation usually starting with, "Mom guess what he did today?" Whenever I was at my son's school, this child was often sitting in the office, unable to attend recess or parties in the classroom because of behavior. He was brought up daily in parent conversation on the playground because he was seen peeing on the school, yelling, swearing and chasing kids around trying to hit them in the privates. After school he never seemed to have anyone to go to and ran around with zero supervision. I often wondered about him, knowing that something wasn't quite right. One day I pulled up after school and saw his father screaming vulgar words at him as he sped off before the kid closed the back car door. I knew I had troubled kids and families at my school too, so it wasn't surprising to me. I knew that our troubled kids and families received more attention to detail than the average family because they needed the support. I figured this was happening at my son's school too. Without a doubt, there are kids at our schools that we keep a closer eye on for so many reasons. I wasn't understanding how this child wasn't one of them. He fell through the cracks. My heart was sick for this child too.

I called a meeting with my son's school administration hoping they could answer some questions and we could feel some emotional relief. At the meeting, there was no responsibility taken or accountability to be had. I was told they would "just keep suspending the offender" to keep him out of school. The principal told me this child should have been hospitalized during kindergarten because of his behavior. I learned this child kissed girls in the reading corner, told them they were sexy and they had nice butts. He would hide in the school, steal and lie to his teachers. I learned that any adult from the neighborhood could come supervise at recess. I discovered that the school doors were open during recess and the supervisors had no accountability of kids' whereabouts during the recess lunch hour. As I asked more questions, I was learning that this administration had no idea what happened inside or outside, nor was any protocol followed for the safety of the kids. As we continued our sleepless nights in our home, I started to second guess everything about this school and how they operated. My husband and I decided that there was no way I could continue my career in Chicago because our children could no longer attend school in the city. We decided I had to resign at the end of the school year and move our family elsewhere.

Since I felt no relief as a parent or an educator, I called our Area Officer which is like a superintendent in the suburbs. She said she was sick about this situation and when she met with the principal he didn't seem to take it very seriously. She shared that he didn't file the proper paperwork at the district office, nor was he aware of all of the facts. She said she would do all she could to get this kid removed from the school on an emergency placement so my son could feel safe. I told her my heart was broken for my son and also for the other kid. I shared that I didn't understand why this child wasn't getting the proper attention he was seeking because he was showing so many red flags. For a five-year-old child to display such behaviors was far from typical. She apologized telling me that as a mother, she couldn't imagine what our family was going through.

I was frantic because nothing was changing. The only person I heard from was the school nurse calling to tell me to come pick up my son because his stomach hurt. I would arrive at school to find him in a sobbing heap on the floor. One of his teachers emailed me telling me that my son was too sensitive in class and that he wasn't completing his work on time. The email was like getting stabbed in the heart. She had no idea what we were going through at home, even though we tried desperately to communicate with the school. She had no idea how trauma changes the brain, behavior and priorities of a child. Another teacher called to tell me she was so sorry and wanted to know what she could do to help him. I was so grateful for her.

I decided to attend the Local School Council meeting (school board meeting) and ask publicly what was being done regarding the safety of our children. At this point rumors were spreading about my child, so I felt if they weren't going to address it, I was. I was an assistant principal one mile away and the unconcerned attitude I received from the school and district blew my mind. How were non-educator parents being treated when issues arose with their kids?

I spoke publicly, not sharing details about what happened to my son, just that the safety of our kids was at risk and I wanted to know what was being done about it. I could barely get the words out of my mouth as people stared at me in disbelief. The principal apologized for the "mishap" and said he was going to form a team of Chicago police officers to create a safety plan for the school. After the meeting, a teary mom came up to me and asked if a certain student was involved in what I was talking about. She named the kid and I said yes. She grabbed my arm and said, "Oh my God, we need to talk. I reported this kid twice for touching my son and I believe the same thing happened to your son." This mother told me that the same kid touched her son twice before our situation started...once in the bathroom and once on the playground. She reported both, the first in writing and the second one with a phone call to the principal. Nothing was done.

After many weeks of insistence, the offender was sent to another Chicago Public School no more than two miles away. Within one week he had an IEP with an eligibility of emotional disability. At that time, in my 12 years as an educator, no Chicago Public School student ever just got an IEP. For a child to get services, we held many meetings, compiled more data than imaginable and we provided interventions for six to twelve weeks, but that was not the case. Again, this child slipped through the cracks. Rumors began and parents from the new school called me asking if what they heard was true. No one had any idea of how true it all was. News stations were calling me asking me to talk about what I knew. I always declined. A group of parents from the offender's new school asked to meet with me. They felt they weren't being told the truth about why the new kid was followed around by a large man in a bright orange jacket that read SECURITY on the back. They weren't told the truth which caused more angst among parents.

Our son's health and our family's healing was at the forefront of our minds at all times, but it feels like your heart is being continuously electrocuted when something horrible happens to your child. We decided to call an attorney after all because so much of what we were dealing with could have been avoided. After meeting with five attorneys, we found one that said he would take the case. He was the only one not afraid of the Chicago Public School system. I could write another book on the seven and a half year legal struggle we endured and how relentless and cruel the defense attorneys and system were, but that's for another time. At the end of the day no one took accountability for this. The reason I'm not going to go into this any further is that as frustrating, painful and unbelievable of an experience it was, none of it matters. Our goal was, is and will always be to take care of our son.

We barely made it through the school year. I resigned. Our home sold. We said good-bye to our neighbors tearfully telling them what we could. We found a house to move into and a school to attend. I interviewed for my first principal job throwing up in the parking lot before I walked in. I was so worried about finances and knew I needed a job similar to the job I had before. I got the job and put on an exterior that was tough as nails, yet I was dying inside.

We moved in August, one day before I started my new principal position and two weeks before my kids started at their new school. Moving brought guilt of taking my third grade daughter away from all of her friends she had since she was a little girl. The worry of continued school refusal for my middle son & the baby starting kindergarten without preschool and neighborhood friends. Leaving our loving neighbors behind. The stress of boxes everywhere and a horrific unsettling in my heart. Yet somehow, with a head of fog, I pushed on.

At our new school we were welcomed by the principal, social worker and his unbelievable second grade teacher. She was one of the most amazing teachers I've ever seen. Mrs. Sobon loved him as she did every child. She possessed excellent teaching skills, but she loved first which is the key to reaching "Those Kids" and all kids for that matter.

My son experienced continuous school refusal, stomach aches and difficulty trusting and making friends. He continued feeling anxious, sad and shameful. He had difficulty falling and staying asleep because thoughts would run rampant in his mind. I was called daily from the school as I tried to run my own school. He missed tons of math because that was therapy time and he still struggles with math to this day. We continued therapy and tried to treat each day as a new one. Our new grade school was a better place. We ran into many teachers who wanted to teach him regardless of his struggles and we had some who did not understand that my son needed a solid, loving and trusting relationship before curriculum. He was just surviving and when you are surviving, math and reading aren't that important to you.

As junior high came, so did a school change & a flood of hormones. With the elementary schools joining into one middle school, it seemed there were more kids who didn't understand him and lots of teachers who misunderstood him. Yes, he needed an education, but attempting to cram academic expectations into the head of a traumatized kid without love and compassion is recipe for disaster. After much frustration we got him a 504 and then an IEP. Those pieces of paper weren't for my son. They were for the teachers who didn't think he needed any special treatment. It makes me sad that some educators need an IEP to treat people as individuals. Incredibly, some still didn't follow his IEP. It stated clearly he needed to sit in the back of class because he thought everyone knew what happened to him. In survival mode, he felt everyone was looking at him and talking about him. One teacher continued to sit him in front to assure that he paid attention to her lesson. Another called him out in front of the class when he said he needed to go to the office and call home. It was written in his IEP that when he needed a break to call home or visit the counselor, there were no questions asked. In front of the class she told him he didn't need to leave and it wasn't a big deal. He started hiding in school so he didn't have to deal with some of his teachers. We lived, we learned, we struggled and we trudged on.

The greatest teachers in middle school advocated for him. They cared more about him than what they were trying to teach him, and most of all showed love and compassion. In their classes he felt like he mattered. They stayed calm when he got upset. They did not question when he needed extra time to complete an assignment. They called to check on him after a bad day. Mrs. Genke, his social worker, was someone we couldn't live without. She understood. She advocated. She built self-esteem. She loved him as a kid, not just a student. Mrs. Genke had a keen understanding that this was a journey, not a destination and she did what she could to instill this in his teachers. One of his ELA teachers, Mrs Turk, who cared greatly for him lost her mother on a Friday afternoon. My son heard of this and asked if he could bake her brownies. As a 6th grader struggling to get to school everyday, he baked his teacher brownies, cut them, covered them with tinfoil and delivered them to her house with a handmade sympathy note. She cared about him and he felt it. He appreciated it and he did anything he could to please her. He felt he mattered in her class.

It wasn't like that in every class, though. Junior high was a nightmare. His life was threatened in 6th grade because a group of boys didn't like that his friends were girls. They commented daily about his longer hair and feminine traits. Each day at lunch he heard different versions of, "I'm gonna kill you faggot." He sat by girls at lunch and worked with girls in class. He expressed to us that he didn't trust boys. He said he was afraid of a group of students who lashed out at him in the hallways, on social media and at lunch each day. My husband and I worked with him to ignore the kids. We reached out to the school for some help and guidance. Mrs. Genke listened and tried to convey the need for more support during unstructured times. This went on for a very long time with meetings and emails and phone calls with the school. It got to the point where our son couldn't get out of bed and go to school. He told us he felt like he was drowning and couldn't function. He was anxious, discouraged, slipping and we were five years into our journey.

His therapist suggested we take him to a behavioral hospital for an intake. This was one of the scariest days of my life. Holding back tears, we took him because we needed help. He was so depressed and desperate for some emotional relief. We all were. He attended a daily program at the hospital to work on coping skills and anxiety relief along with assignments from school. He worked with kids who were suicidal, cutters, had eating disorders and many other emotional challenges. He stayed in the program for six weeks. He seemed a bit less restless and had more tools to cope with his feelings and other kids' behavior. He was prescribed medication to help stabilize his emotions. He reentered school with the support of his social worker. It was a difficult transition back especially because he was more worried about surviving the day than he was about school work. In all honesty, I was more concerned about some of his teachers' reactions to him than I was about him. Their relationship with him was more important than ever during this transition.

At this time, I was doing my best to run my own school. Trying to give teachers and students all they needed to be successful but I was really feeling worn down. I always put on a tenacious front, but I was on very thin emotional ice every day. The demands of a school principal mixed with the overwhelming demands of my family was getting to be too much.

With a great deal of therapy and medication, we survived 6th grade. At this time I told my husband I was struggling badly at work but I hid it very well. I felt a great deal of resentment because I was spending so much time taking care of other people's kids and was struggling to take care of my own. It was so unnatural for me to feel such sadness. It was depressing and draining to feel like I had to fight for happiness every single day. Every time my son struggled, it felt like a little piece of me died and that has never stopped.

We toyed with changing schools for our son, but continued to come back to the fact that he needed to get through issues and not run away. That attitude lasted one more year. After 7th grade, that was it. This junior high school was not a positive match for our son. The culture was not what we needed for our son to thrive. Fully aware that changing schools for an 8th grade kid was insane, it couldn't be more insane that our lives had become. We needed a fresh start.

We enrolled him in a private school in another town. He was scared and we were too, but hopeful for a new beginning. There has been nothing simple about this whole process, but there was some relief at the new school. The kids in general were kind, had manners and ignorance was not tolerated. He had a better year in 8th grade and it was the best parenting decision we ever made. Taking leaps of faith are sometimes the only option left.

The summer before his 8th grade year, I was preparing to take a leap of faith as well. I was on the verge of a nervous breakdown. After a 6th year serving as principal, I decided that I needed to regain some control over my life and focus 100% on my family. I resigned my principal position and wanted to start my own business to help educators understand trauma and work with kids who struggle. I wanted to create and deliver keynotes about our story and how we can live through anything and come out stronger. I wanted to develop practical strategies to help educators with things they were never taught, but expected to implement. After a 20 year career, I was terrified of the pay cut, but at the end of the day it didn't matter. I would no longer be paying into my pension, but that didn't matter either. My livelihood and health were on the line & so was my family's stability. I jumped. I took a leap of faith and I jumped. I continue to search for inner peace and work through family issues to raise happy, healthy and productive citizens of this ever changing world. Teaching "Those Kids" isn't easy. Raising "Those Kids" isn't easy either, but nothing worth it is ever easy. My kid is one of "Those Kids" and he is amazing.

# Invictus

Out of the night that covers me,
Black as the pit from pole to pole,
I thank whatever gods may be
For my unconquerable soul.

In the fell clutch of circumstance
I have not winced nor cried aloud.
Under the bludgeoning of chance
My head is bloody, but unbowed.

Beyond this place of wrath and tears
Looms but the Horror of the shade,
And yet the menace of the years
Finds and shall find me unafraid.

It matters not how strait the gate,
How charged with punishments the scroll,
I am the master of my fate,
I am the captain of my soul.

-Willian Ernest Henley

# Raising one of "Those Kids" takeaways

- Nothing prepares you for parenting.

- Nothing prepares you for teaching. Always put Compassion before Curriculum, Relationships before Rigor and Kids First.

- Every parent/guardian does the best they can with what they know.

- Trauma is difficult for the entire family. Parents & siblings need compassion too.

- Read 504s and IEPs. Ask questions and work with parents to hear their story.

- Never be afraid. You're never alone even though it feels that way sometimes.

- Follow your gut. If something doesn't seem right with a child's behavior, you're probably right.

- If someone doesn't listen to your concerns about a child, keep going until someone does.

- Know that everyone you meet has something they're struggling with.

- Empathy is an amazing thing for educators to learn:

- According to nursing scholar, Theresa Wiseman, there are four qualities of empathy:

- **<u>PERSPECTIVE TAKING</u>**

  ✳ Your reality is your perspective. Seeing things from another's perspective is essential to understanding "Those Kids." It's almost impossible to understand "Those Kids" if we close our minds to what life is like outside of our own.

- **<u>STAY OUT OF JUDGEMENT</u>**

  ✳ Instead of judging behavior and families, what if we replaced judgement with curiosity and asked questions to learn more about the why behind behavior. That way we can be a part of the solution and not a part of the problem.

- **<u>RECOGNIZE EMOTION IN OTHERS</u>**

  ✳ Recognize emotion in our kids. Realize the complexity of the trauma cycle. Recognize signs in your students. Respond with curiosity, love, compassion and hope. Reflect on what is in your control.

- **<u>COMMUNICATING</u>**

  ✳ Communicate that you see your kids. You see the struggle. You want to help. Build self-esteem and know that with "Those Kids" Compassion must come before Curriculum.

# "Those Kids" Need You

As educators, sometimes we feel like we have to fix every child. We stand in front of our classes and see so many different needs. Please take those weights out of your backpack because we don't have to fix every child. I would argue that you can't. I can't fix my son, which is heartbreaking. I'm a mom, a teacher, a school administrator & I fix things. I've had to learn that with my (AWE) Actions, Words & Expressions I can help guide him through the wild current of life, which is much more powerful than fixing him or anyone else.

The ups.

The downs.

The uncertainty.

The sleepless nights.

The kids who don't understand.

The adults who misunderstand.

The overwhelming expectations.

The swirling thoughts.

The loss of confidence.

The loss of vulnerability.

The loss of joy.

The depression.

The anxiety.

The loneliness.

The tears.

The worry.

The reclaiming of his life.

# This is why we need you.

I've shared with my own children that when they're born, they sit in a canoe with us and we take the lead, guiding them from the rear through the current of life. They live, they learn, they experience and develop perspective of success, failure, loss & love. As time goes on, we begin to switch spots sliding past each other during adolescence and teen years and eventually they take the spot in back of their life canoes. As parents, we observe from the front cheering them on as they learn from mistakes, celebrate successes and ultimately take charge of their own lives. Some kids have a lot of guidance veering in and out of life's snags and some don't. As educators, we have to remember that kids don't come with instructions. Parents and caretakers do the best they can with what they know. Some kids show up in boats alone. They do what they can to navigate life's expectations. Some of their parents are still alone in their vessels as well. Some come with lots of money in their canoes and some with holes in the bottom. Some canoes are fancy and others worn down. Some have seen the world and others have never been out of their neighborhood waters. The water they float through can be beautifully clean or awfully muddy. **We have no control of how they come, where they come from and how much guidance they have. We do however, have control of practicing perspective and helping them work through the snags of life. What a beautiful opportunity.**

In reality, students come to us with a wide variety of learning levels and styles. They are socially diverse and emotionally unique. Some have been through traumatic experiences such as physical, emotional or sexual abuse, neglect, terrorism, bullying, divorcing parents, terminal illness, rape, drug addiction and so much more. Now we can add pandemic and national unsettlement to the list. Some sell drugs and are making more money than their teachers, so why stop? Some have two loving parents, some have just a grandparent, some have a guardian and some live in foster care. Some play violent video games and watch inappropriate movies and others are very sheltered. Some hear I love you and get hugs daily, some never experience either. Our system expects they all perform up to "standards" even though there's nothing standard about their lives. I hope one positive outcome of Covid-19 is that being vulnerable comes much easier for all of us. During this time, so many lost their jobs, loved ones, homes, businesses and many lost hope. Kids were taught at home by their parents/guardians and teachers taught through a computer screen. We were asked to wear masks and stay six feet apart. Together, we were all vulnerable.

Educators take great pride in helping kids learn, grow, build confidence and strive for excellence. I've worked with kids from all walks of life and understand each has a heart, soul and tremendous longing to matter in the eyes of others. They want connection, guidance and love. Regardless if we are teaching in person with or without masks or teaching through virtual learning, connection must be our top priority. Our kids will always be far from robots, although our education system seems to think they all squeak and beep simultaneously. To me, teaching and learning has always been a problem-solving cycle powered by strong relationships. The power of a smile, an arm around a shoulder, a note of encouragement, the modification of time. The power to listen, to love and to understand. The power of instilling hope in a child, encouraging a child, building a child's self-esteem. The power that HE knows YOU believe in HIM is the greatest gift of all.

## This is why we need you.

The reason I shared my story is because my son needs all of you and so do I. He needs you to help him trust again, love and persevere. I need your kindness and compassion so I can trust again. He needs you to understand why he is withdrawn and gets sick to his stomach. I need you to be patient, understanding and interested in our healing. He needs you to understand why homework doesn't interest him, & how he has difficulty participating in activities. I need you to be open to growth and understand that our kids are not just test scores. He needs you to understand that sometimes he could care less about the grades assigned to him because he's just not available to care. I need you to realize that my son's mental health is more important than the grades he receives. He needs your help with peers, because his years of natural peer interaction were robbed from him. Some nights he doesn't get much sleep because of anxiety. Some mornings he struggles to get out of bed because he suffers from depression. I need you to smile, give me a hug, hold my hand and refrain from judging my parenting.

My son has always had a supportive canoe guiding him through the wild current of life. Two loving and educated parents and two beautiful siblings. A house. Two cars. Two dogs. As wonderful as that scenario may sound, we struggle. A lot. But we continue to rise above because of the power of perspective. There are so many kids sitting in our classrooms that walk through struggle alone. For every child, every parent, every caretaker, every sibling please know…

# This is why we need you.

My main goal is to help you understand how your AWE has an astonishing impact on the life journey of a child. We are not robots, even though society likes to tell us we are. We are unique & amazing individuals just waiting for someone to help us shine through the sameness.

We live in a world where children come into our lives homeless, depressed, anxious, abused, and/or mentally ill. Some suffer from Post-Traumatic Stress Disorder (PTSD), have a disease, have a special need, have an incarcerated parent, live in an alcoholic household, have a parent or a sibling addicted to drugs. Some have a parent being deported, while others have a dying parent…the list is endless. But believe me, you can help. Our kids need you. I need you. We all need you.

This book teaches how to be the difference-maker in a child's life. Learn about the importance of building relationships & school culture and realize that practicing positive AWE makes it happen. You will walk away with strategies to work with "Those Kids" & most of all be given the time to practice perspective.

Watching my child suffer has been the most difficult thing I've ever been through. It's also an honor being his mom and helping him navigate the challenges.

When my son was 12 years old, he drew this depiction of his life:

He said no matter how hard he tries, he feels weighed down by what happened to him. He said that teachers just don't understand and the pressure to perform is overwhelming. He shared that he is not lazy, but he's not always capable of doing everything perfect as expected and on teacher timelines.

Please think of this drawing and the strategies I share in all of your interactions with students. "Those Kids" will always be in our schools. "Those Kids" need our patience, understanding and kindness. They need us to see things from their perspective so they feel like they matter. Know that in all you do and all you say you are working with someone's child and your AWE can help kids soar, or add weight to their shackles. Understand that "Those Kids" are OUR Kids and spread that message in all you do.

Every child deserves a champion – an adult who will never give up on them, who understands the power of connection, and insists that they become the best that they can possibly be. Teachers become great actors and great actresses. ... We come to work when we don't feel like it, and we're listening to policy that doesn't make sense – and we teach anyway.

-Rita Pierson

# "Those Kids" Need You takeaways

- Kids gain confidence from us. Traumatized kids, misunderstood kids and kids who take frequent detours from what's expected are searching for people who believe in them.

- When kids act out, there is always a reason. Take the opportunity to search for it.

- There's no such thing as a bad kid.

- We can't fix kids. We can, however, take the time to understand the why behind behavior in order to guide kids on their journeys. That one positive, helpful, compassionate adult makes such a difference.

- Tell kids how proud you are...even if it's a small accomplishment.

- Make sure each child knows he/she matters in your class.

- Every child wants to matter in your class.

- Never lose sight of the reason you became an educator.

- Perspective is so important. Know that he is having a hard time. He's not giving you a hard time.

- Your mission as an educator is SO important. Thank you!

# PRACTICAL STRATE-GIES & STORIES TO HELP ALL EDUCATORS HELP THOSE KIDS

# $\mathcal{A}$cknowledge before $\mathcal{A}$ccusation

Regardless of our actions and behavior, we all search for validation. When working to build relationships with our kids, especially the challenging ones, validation is essential. Kids who take frequent detours from what's expected often feel "in trouble" regardless of what they've done. They hear the phrase, "What did you do?" so often that even when they didn't do anything, they still feel like they're "bad." It becomes a habit to feel in trouble, to feel inferior and to feel discouraged. A huge part of our mission as kid-builders is to provide opportunities to help them build self-esteem, understand natural consequences and know they can rise above. Tweaking our vocabulary is one step we can practice to positively impact their journeys. For example, instead of using the phrases, good behavior and bad behavior, we can switch to expected and unexpected behavior. If a student is running around the classroom, he/she can be told his/her behavior is unexpected instead of telling the child they're bad. If a student is running around outside at recess, we can tell the student their behavior is expected, instead of telling the child they're good. Everything we say and do shapes the kind of relationships we build with kids & ultimately shapes their self worth.

When working through behavior, think Acknowledge before Accusation and take a look at the following practices:

## Due Process

In order to feel validated, we want our kids to be heard. Even when we do something we shouldn't, being heard is part of the growing and learning process. The words we use when speaking and listening to kids are vital to the outcome of the situation. How and where we offer kids a chance to share their side is part of relationship building. Do we take time to listen in a private place and really hear what they're telling us? Do we validate their feelings and thoughts? Do we guide them in making better choices? Or do we settle on writing a referral and kicking them out? Offering our students the opportunity to share their side of the story is acknowledging them. They need to be heard and we need to listen.

## Word Choice

Words are part of our AWE and our AWE determines how we build rapport and relationships with our kids. Word choice plays a huge role in determining how any interaction with a student will unfold. Those who are often in trouble already feel paranoid they're always doing something wrong. Instead of saying, "I am not happy with your behavior!" say, "How do you think your behavior might affect other people in this class?"

Never be afraid to ask what happened. Acknowledge before Accusation. The words we use to find out what happened impact the direction of the situation with our students. For example, we could say, "What did you do?" which seems accusatory in nature. Or, we could ask, "Hey bud, can you please tell me what happened?" Both phrases offer time for the student to tell her story. Asking for the story instead of accusing is key when activating strategies of Acknowledge before Accusation. Think about the openness of asking for the story instead of assuming that the kid misbehaved in some way. With time, kids whose behaviors are misunderstood can become more clear with understanding, validation and acknowledgement from the adults around them. This is especially true with kids who have experienced trauma.

When my son was a freshman in high school, he was called to the dean's office and told to sit down. The dean said, "At this school, we respect security. Looks like this morning you didn't show respect to security and you need to apologize." My son said his heart started to beat really fast and he felt angry because he didn't know what the dean was talking about. He told her that he wasn't disrespectful to anyone that morning. The dean insisted he go out and apologize to the security guard. He went into the hall and told the security guard he was sorry, but he didn't know what he was sorry for. The security guard said, "Wait. What? Are you in trouble? It wasn't you I was talking about." My son went back to the dean and was visibly upset by this situation. The dean asked how the apology went and he said fine. She said, "Well I don't think it went fine by the attitude you are showing." She then dismissed him from her office. When he left her office, he texted me in all caps (and we all know what that means) how angry he was because he felt he was yelled at and accused of something he didn't do. He was triggered and set off by an adult who accused him before acknowledging him. We need the opposite. I called the dean to ask about the situation. She reminded me that she was the disciplinarian and she was here to help in any way that she could. I shared that I respect her position, but starting a conversation with accusing before acknowledging adds fuel to the fire. She shared that she looked into it more and found out that it wasn't my son and that it was a misunderstanding. Unfortunately, the damage was done. Traumatized kids are often misunderstood and take frequent detours from what is expected. They often struggle to regain regulation when Accusation comes before Acknowledgement. A child who has experienced trauma already has a backpack filled with anxious emotions and if the words and tone appear accusatory, it automatically adds fuel to any interaction. We don't want to add stress to the already compromised child and situation. To build relationships with kids, they need to feel that we are genuinely interested in hearing their story. That takes time, love, compassion and the perspective that building a trusting relationship with this child will certainly help him/her grow to be better. It takes guts as educators to look in the mirror and say, man, maybe it's something I am doing that is setting this kid off. Along with offering the child a chance to speak, carefully choosing our words determines how conversations will unfold with our kids. Think about how differently this could have been handled if the dean said, "Good morning! Hey who did you walk into school with this morning? Were there any issues with security?" Word choice is everything.

You don't have to see the whole staircase, just take the first step.

-Martin Luther King, Jr.

## Acknowledge before Accusation take-aways

- Validation is something we all search for.

- Acknowledge the situation before accusing anyone of anything.

- Kids are not bad. Their behavior may be undesired, but as humans, they are not bad.

- Replace "What did you do?" with "Tell me what happened."

- You are in control of your Actions, Words & Expressions (AWE).

# $\mathcal{B}$onfire $\mathcal{B}$ehavior

Behavior is like a roaring bonfire and there are several things that spark the fire & get it going. Frequently, it's our AWE (Actions, Words and Expressions) that fans or extinguishes the flames. Taking personal accountability for your AWE is the start to growth in this area of working with tough kids.

Controlling our Actions, Words, and Expressions allow us to take ownership of our conversations. How we talk to people matters! It takes time to practice perspective on this issue, but can alleviate so many problems in our classrooms, in our schools and in our society. At the end of the day each of us is either a part of the problem or a part of the solution. Behavior comes in many forms. We have to practice understanding the why behind the behavior, addressing the underlying causes & teaching behavior we want to see. Those actions build relationships. Those relationships, in turn, minimize behaviors because when kids feel supported, loved and understood they are much better suited to comply with what's expected.

Below you will find insight on the power of our Actions, Words, and Expressions that can either result in adding fuel to the fire, or calming and ultimately extinguishing it.

**"You don't have your homework, again?"**
The ongoing debate of whether or not kids should have homework. Homework is neither good nor bad, but we need to consider that we're all unique and have different needs in order to feel successful. Einstein once said, "The definition of insanity is doing the same thing over and over again and expecting a different result." For example...We assign homework to Gabriel. He doesn't do it. We get mad. We assign more homework. Gabriel doesn't do it. We get angry. We assign more homework. Gabriel doesn't do it. We get frustrated. We assign more homework. Gabriel still does not do it. This scenario plays out in classrooms on a daily basis.

It is so important to think about the purpose of homework. Do we assign it so we can get a grade in the grade book, because we think teachers are supposed to, or is there a specific purpose/outcome? Thinking about student circumstances is important, too. Sometimes "Those Kids" are not available to do homework for many reasons. Know their stories and do whatever you can to help them feel success. Even in a two-parent, well-educated family, homework can pose stress. Kids are involved in many outside activities and they are in school all day long. How much is too much? In homes where support is not a reality, homework is not a priority. If we can practice our perspective and realize that every house is different, perhaps we can think about who benefits from homework and who doesn't. This does not mean to lower expectations. Instead, be sure the expectations are achievable and designed to make the student feel good about himself.

**"Late. Why are you always late?"**
Oftentimes, it's not a child's fault for showing up tardy to school. What AWE do we use when kids are late to our classes? It is important to pay attention to how tardy kids are treated in the office when they arrive because this is where school culture begins. Does the secretary smile and welcome the child, or is the child met with, "Late again?" Usually there is a reason when a student frequents the tardy sign-in sheet. Being productive means talking with the child and getting his/her story behind the tardiness. As both a teacher and administrator, I had the opportunity to have many conversations during student arrival and I will always remember Martin. Martin was in fourth grade and came to school late at least three times per week at different points in the school year. One morning I walked Martin to class and asked if he had a minute. His response was, "What do you want?" I invited him to sit down in the hall with me. I asked him how things were going with his grandma and he asked me why I cared. I shared that I knew grandma was taking care of him and I wanted to see if I could help him get to school on time. Martin started to get really upset and said to me, "You know I sleep on the couch right? You know the cat pees on the couch right? You know my mom is in jail again right? You know my grandma can't walk right?" I told him I was so sorry to hear about his mom and that I didn't know he slept on the couch. I told him that I wanted to help him. He asked if I could talk to his grandma, but warned me that his grandma sleeps a lot so

she might not answer the phone. I laughed a little and told him that my grandma sleeps a lot too. I shared that I would call grandma and touch base with him at recess and I did. Follow-through with all kids is essential for building relationships, especially "Those Kids."

Martin's mom was in and out of jail and his patterns of attendance fluctuated depending on when she was home or away. Dad wasn't in the picture. Martin ate cereal with water each morning and if mom wasn't there to get him on the bus, he didn't get on the bus.

After talking with the student, circle back with the parent or guardian. Although not all solutions come from approaching the home situation, we certainly have to try. Opening up dialogue with a parent/guardian and offering help shows that we care and want to be a part of the solution. I called grandma and here was our conversation:

Me: Good morning Mrs. Malczk, it's Mrs. LaFleur, how are you?
Grandma: Oh Mrs. LaFleur my daughter is back in jail and I worry about Martin. I can't keep up with him. He runs from me and I am so tired.
Me: Mrs. Malczk, I'm so sorry to hear about you daughter. I was wondering if I could help you get Martin to school. He does so well when he's here and perhaps we can help with the morning routine.
Grandma: That would help so much, please help me.
Me: We will help you and we will have someone on the bus to greet him each morning starting with me.

For one week, I rode the bus and let Martin know that I would be waiting for him.

When a child comes late to school, the hope is that he/she is greeted with a welcome. When a child walks late into class, the hope is that he/she is greeted with a smile, told quietly where we are in the lesson and we move on. We can also tell the student she was missed which is relationship building at its best.

The same expectations can be put in place for older kids. Junior high and high school kids who frequent the tardy sign-in sheet have a reason. When we build relationships by asking questions because we genuinely care and show the desire to alleviate distress, we make progress. Older kids express many things by showing an increased pattern of tardiness. Kids of all ages will open up if the trusting relationship is alive and well, but we will continue to receive a serious attitude from the kid who doesn't feel we believe in him. This can't be a surprise, because it's the reality of kids who are traumatized, misunderstood and those who take frequent detours from what's expected.

**"Put your hood down."**
When kids misbehave they are usually trying to communicate. When a student has his hood up it can mean a lot of different things such as lack of confidence, sadness, anger, feeling unsafe & insecure and even identity.

Telling a kid to put her hood down may not go well unless we first establish rapport with the student. I was consulting in a northern suburb of Chicago and helped transition a student back to school after a 10-day suspension. The student was in 7th grade and always wore a hood. He was frequently told to remove his hood and would shut down. This led to frustrated teachers and constant power struggles. The first move I made was just talking with the student to get a feel for his interests. I asked if it was ok to pull up a chair next to him and he said yes. When we talked, we were always eye to eye. We talked about video games, rappers and wrestling for over an hour. I asked him if he knew any old school wrestlers like Hulk Hogan or Jake "the snake" Roberts and he started naming so many wrestlers that I couldn't keep up. This connection started our relationship. For over an hour we discussed Jimmy "Superfly" Snuka jumping off the top turnbuckle and the cars he loved in Grand Theft Auto. As we talked, I would ask questions about what he was reading or what the teacher assigned him. We would sneak expected work into our conversations. After a few days together, I asked why he wore the hood. He said it made him feel safe. He told me that his father died right before school started and he found his grandfather unresponsive in his car in February. He said he stays up all night and plays video games or watches YouTube and that's why he falls asleep in school. He shared that he worries about his mom all the time. I look at a kid like this and am grateful that he is in school. With or without a hood, he comes. That is a win. Together, we created a chart of hood zones and no hood zones and we practiced and talked about why certain places would be better without a hood. It took a week of practice and prep, but he did it. PE, STEM, lunch and hallways were no hoodie zones and he complied most of the time. Instead of verbals, we privately held up a small card that showed a hood down. He believed he mattered and all he needed was an adult who understood his story.

**"Move your clip up/down."**
Imagine for a second if your principal posted your evaluation in the main hallway of the school for all to see. Imagine being forced to clip up when you succeeded and down when you didn't. Now imagine it was all done in front of your peers. Yikes! Clip charts can cause public humiliation and that doesn't always end well with kids, especially "Those Kids."

As a principal, I was frequently called to Alison's kindergarten classroom for assistance with Antoni. Upon arrival he was often face down on the floor sobbing loudly. The teacher would say to me, "Heidy, here he goes again. I can't teach when he's like this." The teacher was frustrated, Antoni was frustrated and I was frustrated. There was a clear pattern that when Antoni's clip was moved down, he lost control. He cried, screamed and sometimes made himself so upset that he threw up. He would also shut down by crawling under a table or cabinet and refusing to talk. This would last for over an hour and many times involved a trip to the sensory room to calm down.

Alison was a great teacher. She knew the curriculum and exposed kids to so many academic opportunities. I had to figure out how to help her understand that Antoni was not responding to the form of behavior modification in her classroom. We had many conversations and I remember this one most:

Me: Alison, let's talk about Antoni's outburst and what frustrates you.
Alison: Yeah. He doesn't do what I ask and I move his clip down and he goes crazy. I need him to do what I say so I can teach him.

Me: I hear you talking about him doing what you say, but don't hear you talking about what he needs. What are the expectations for him?

Alison: When I call kids to the carpet, he needs to come and sit with his legs crossed. He needs to be quiet so I can teach and he can learn.

Me: We know he is diagnosed with ADHD. Does he have the same expectations as the other kids?

Alison: Yes, they all have the same expectations.

Me: I wonder if we can work with him on a different expectation system that's not public because the piece that seems to set him off is the chart. I understand that you want him to listen and do work, but right now something has to change.

Alison: Heidy I've always used a chart. I don't know what else to use.


In tears, Alison got to a point that is difficult for a lot of us. The feeling of not knowing what to do. We worked together with the OT, his special education teacher and his mom to establish a system where we were working on one behavior at a time. Alison felt better because she wasn't losing Antoni several times a day and we were helping him progress by focusing less on the public clip chart and more on his individual needs. Academics are always important, but for Antoni feeling safe and secure had to come well before any other expectations. Our AWE has a direct impact on any behavioral situation and ultimately someone's life journey.


It's not what you look at that matters, it's what you see.

-Henry David Thoreau

The Bonfire Behavior full page resource is featured in the Those Kids Study Guide which is available as an instant download on my website for $15.
Visit www.heidylafleur.com or scan here:

**Bonfire Behavior take-aways**

- Behavior is like a bonfire. Our AWE can either accelerate it or calm it.

- When we handle behavior, we are either part of the problem or part of the solution.

- In homes where support is not a reality, homework is not a priority.

- Balance what you need with what the student needs. Connection. Connection. Connection.

- You are in control of your Actions, Words & Expressions (AWE).

# Compassion before Curriculum

According to Merriam-Webster this is the definition of *compassion:*

**sympathetic consciousness of others' distress together with a desire to alleviate it**

The desire to alleviate it. This is the foundation of the greatest relationship building block in the world. As a principal, I had many opportunities to highlight compassion as a building block for our school community. I recall when Becky, a beautiful 29 year old mother of two, was diagnosed with breast cancer. We did all we could to listen, love and understand. After meeting with mom and dad, I assured them we would take care of their kindergartner, Mia. The parents were unsure, scared, faithful and positive. As Mia smiled her way through the hallways, her academic focus was foggy. She was surviving. With mom sick at home, school became an escape for her and it was our job to help her through this tough time. She cried a lot wondering why her mommy was changing so much. Mom was bloated from the steroids, her hair was falling out and she was exhausted.

Mia started her day with our social worker. They practiced positive words and happy thoughts to start her day and together they walked to class and had a conversation with her teacher. Each day, this worked for Mia to feel supported. As a team, we worked to support Mia both academically and emotionally.

After a double mastectomy and months of treatment, mom was cancer-free, but the relief did not last long. This time the cancer was in her brain. She became really sick and I heard concerns from teachers about Mia not doing her homework. Her reading and math were both lagging and there was concern she would continue to fall behind. I assured the concerned teachers that while academic skills are always important, their best strategy was love and under-standing. She would learn her sounds, her letters and she would learn how to read.

One Friday in late May, I pulled Mia aside to ask how we could help. She said she wished her mom could see the deck. I did not understand so I continued to ask more questions. Mia shared her mom wanted a deck on the back of their house and her dad was building it. She repeatedly said that she wished the deck was done so her mom could sit out there.

I decided to call the mayor to ask for help. I asked to use city equipment and city workers who might volunteer. He agreed and things started moving very quickly. I started a Go Fund Me for the family and was blown away at the generosity and love in the community. In one week, the Go Fund Me was over $14,000 and the deck was almost finished. People volunteered, companies and the city donated time, equipment and materials. Neighbors brought food and coolers of beer to share. A designer created an unbelievable living space for this family right outside their back door.

While construction was taking place outside, I visited Becky inside. She was so sick yet so grateful. We held hands and I assured her we would take care of her kids. Compassion before Curriculum always.

The best gift was seeing the heart warming smiles on Mia and her dad's faces. That feeling of compassion, helping, loving and actively seeking to alleviate someone's hurt is incredibly satisfying. Mia's mom saw a glimpse of the deck and passed soon after. Mia learned sounds, letters, and to read. She also took her time and went at her own pace. We focused on her social emotional well being first and academics second. Her timeline was not like everyone else's, but everyone else in that class still had a mom.

It shouldn't matter how slowly a child learns as long as we are encouraging them not to stop.

-Robert John Meehan

## Compassion before Curriculum take-aways

- Experiences and opportunities. That's what it's really about. That's what they'll remember.

- Learning should not be a race. Eventually, we all get there.

- Maslow before Bloom always.

- Never hesitate to advocate for building a social emotional foundation before academic expectations.

- You are in control of your Actions, Words & Expressions (AWE).

# Defiant vs. Deficient

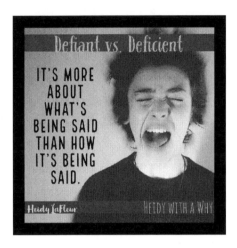

Deficient is defined as lacking in some necessary quality or element while defiant is defined as a disposition to resist: willingness to contend or fight. Often we are quick to judge that a student is defiant. Perhaps the student is deficient in proper love, care or education that has taken him to defiance. Hurt, sad, angry and misunderstood people tend to lash out at other people. One might ask what a defiant child is fighting for. Perhaps it's a voice or permission to be different or understood by adults around them. Maybe they are desperate for someone to listen to their story. Kids come from different places with different circumstances that necessitate the need for different expectations. For some kids staying in school all day is a win because it is better than the abusive home life they frequent. For others, who come from a loving family, scoring well on a math exam and being inducted into the National Honor Society is a win. Regardless, instilling hope and self-esteem is essential to every child no matter their particular circumstance.

All behavior is communication. Acknowledging why people become defiant is the first step to figuring out how to respond to behavior. We cannot change other people's behavior. We can only influence which requires modeling, teaching and helping them effectively deal with anger and frustration. Here are a few favorite strategies for working with defiant kids:

**Use questions instead of statements.**
Questions cannot be argued. Instead of, "I said stop talking," try, "Can you please help me understand why you think it is ok to continue talking while I'm teaching?" By using questions we remove the argument. Instead of, "Don't you dare talk to me like that," try, "Can you please help me understand why you feel you can speak to another person like that?" Realize that defiance happens out of anger and frustration. We don't want to add to their anger and frustration. What we want to do is help them build strategies to release the anger in productive ways.

**Don't take behavior personally.**
Although teaching and learning can get us emotional, don't take student behavior personally. It's not you our kids are after, it's their own hurt causing them to communicate as they do. We don't have to fix them. We have to use strategies to guide them on their journeys. When a student uses a loud tone or rude words when they speak with us, we have to take a breath and remember that it's more about what's being said than how it's being said. Many times, defiant students tell it like it is and it's more about their deficiency in articulating their feelings in an appropriate manner. Our goal is to guide the student on stating their concerns more appropriately which takes practice and patience and time.

**Refuse to believe monkey see, monkey do.**

As a junior high assistant principal, I often had teachers tell me that they would not tolerate defiant students in their classes because then all of the other kids would think they can act that way. The other students are looking at us and how we deal with the defiant behavior. They are not plotting their defiance against the teacher. Most kids who see a student show defiance to an adult are blown away, get wide-eyed and can't even imagine speaking to an adult like that. Solid classroom management, relationship building, using strategies for defiant students and believing in every student to give us their best is more productive than believing monkey see, monkey do.

The kids who need the most love will ask for it in the most unloving ways.

-Russell Barkley

# Defiant vs. Deficient take-aways

- It's more about what's being said than how it's being said.

- All emotions are ok, yet we must teach kids how to work through emotions.

- All behavior is communication.

- It's not you our kids are after, it's their own hurt causing them to communicate as they do.

- You are in control of your Actions, Words & Expressions (AWE).

# $E$mpower over $E$go

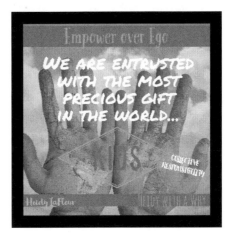

Educators are empowered to make every day a great day for every child. When we think about how many adults are in a school building, we must believe that every adult makes an impact on our students. Where are the administrators, teachers, paraprofessionals, custodians, the nurse, the social worker, etc. during student arrival and dismissal? Where is everyone during passing time? Are we working collectively during non-instructional times to guide our kids in positive and productive ways?

Since strong and trusting relationships are needed for student growth, the goal is for each member of the school community to play a role. Oftentimes, our professional development omits bus drivers, cafeteria workers, and custodians, yet all of them play a powerful role in the relationship building process. These people work with our kids each day and yet, very often we provide little opportunity for them to be part of the collective responsibility and feel an important part of what we do. As a team, our goal is to make every day the best day for every child. That means everyone in the school building has responsibility to build kids up.

## Bus Drivers

I realized quickly as an administrator that I could spend a lot of precious time reviewing and working through bus referrals for seat hopping, disrespect of all sorts, and swearing on the bus. I decided to get out and meet the bus drivers, get on the bus, talk with them, learn about them and invite them to something I called "Donuts with Drivers." Food brings people together and interest in each other brings us even closer. When we met for donuts and discussion, I heard about the hardships of bus driving and some of the kids who were difficult. I learned that it was a second career after retirement for some and for others, their only career. I shared our school mission and vision and asked for their input on how we could improve and what I could do to help them. I let them know how important they were to our kids, parents and school community. They are the first face some of our kids see when they think about school. I invited them to participate in special days and spirit weeks, encouraging each to wear crazy hair or their favorite jersey. The goal was to help drivers understand we are on the same team, supporting each other to support kids. Bus referrals significantly decreased because the foundation was built. The foundation of compassion, relationships, team, and human connection. Each day I would take a minute to talk with every driver to touch base. If there were issues, we game planned and I found myself riding the bus once in a while so the kids knew we were a team and the school bus was an extension of their classrooms. I encouraged our teachers and staff to ride the bus a few times each year as well.

## Custodians

The people we rely on to clean up the mess, put "sawdust" on the puke, cut the grass, clean the corners, prepare the lunchroom and unclog the sink are key when working with hard to reach kids. As a school community, we must make certain they know they matter. Custodians can read to kids, participate in a science experiment and teach kids a great deal about cleanliness and what they can do to help keep the school beautiful.

## Lunch Staff

Those preparing and serving lunch play an integral part of building school culture. Challenge yourself to make sure your lunch staff understands all kids are different. Some won't come with their lunch tickets and some will try to grab more than one milk. If you have students who struggle with the lack of structure during lunchtime, be sure to be the greatest advocate for your kids. Talk with the lunch staff and encourage them to get to know kids personally. Walk through the lunch line once in a while so you can make sure your students, especially "Those Kids" are connecting with the lunch staff in positive ways.

## Nurses/Office Staff

How kids are treated when they go to the nurse or office is critical to building school culture. The office staff and nurses are examples of more people who influence the school culture and therefore are part of the collective responsibility to make every day the best day for every child. The office staff is another first face of the school. They work with administrators, kids, teachers, parents and community members and how they treat people matters. A lot. Walking into the school office and observing language used, along with body language provides great insight into how the school honors relationships.

## Paraprofessionals

Paraprofessionals are some of the most undervalued people in education. These people are often on the front lines with challenging behaviors, yet they receive little training. Administrators and special education teams making decisions about difficult kids without consulting paras makes very little sense. We all have a collective responsibility to be in the know when it comes to planning for our kids. Paraprofessionals are the people we often rely upon to track student data, supervise and monitor, create activities, and interact with our most vulnerable kids. It is crucial that they feel a part of the team. Typically, paraprofessionals work on a different contract than teachers so professional development time doesn't overlap. Do all you can to train paraprofessionals and provide time and opportunity to listen to their opinions. Encourage them and all other adults to build relationships with kids outside of required time. Involve ALL school personnel to assure a collective responsibility to make every day the best day for every child.

Individually, we are one drop. Together, we are an ocean.

-Ryunosuke Satoro

## Empower over Ego take-aways

- We are entrusted with the most precious gift in the world...kids.

- Kids have the greatest chance when schools adopt collective responsibility.

- Culture begins in the school office.

- Every team member must know their role in shaping the lives of our kids.

- You are in control of your Actions, Words & Expressions (AWE).

# $\mathcal{F}$eedback with $\mathcal{F}$eeling

Positive and negative feedback are the foundations for growth. For kids who have been traumatized, misunderstood, or take frequent detours from what is expected, feedback is often negative. Continuous negative feedback sinks in and becomes the kid's identity quickly. When we criticize students we must compliment them at the same time. This builds relationships and connection because adding a bit of humor eases the negative feedback. For example, "Jenny, why are you taking Sam's markers? I heard him tell you twice not to take the markers. By the way, your markers are really cool. Where did you get them?" Feedback is given both verbally and nonverbally through our facial expressions, tone, body language and word usage.

When we know our kids well and take time to hear their stories, we better understand that Feedback with Feeling provides support, empathy and understanding. Kids come to us in many ways, but I like to think about it as students who are ready to learn and students who are merely surviving. Students ready to learn show up ready to learn. They are properly fed, clothed, & come from emotionally stable environments. They already feel like they matter. They are willing to take risks and fail, understanding that failing is a stepping stone on the path to success. They usually have school supplies, and want to please the teacher. The key is that students ready to learn know how to please the teacher. These kids do well with authentic feedback, as they usually don't feel worried or threatened by what we share.

Kids who've been traumatized, misunderstood and those who take frequent detours from what's expected are often just trying to survive. They are in survival mode which makes learning particularly difficult as they are not always available to participate as we would like them to. Some kids just surviving often possess poor nutrition, dirty clothes, and come from unstable home lives. Most feel threatened by feedback or suggestions and are anxious, easily embarrassed, and defensive. They feel they don't matter. The takeaway is that kids who are just surviving want to please the teacher too, but they don't know how. They will get attention however they can. They often are perceived as disrespectful or defiant. Focus your feedback on meeting their basic needs before expecting academics. Instead of expectations for all, being aware that the needs of our students are so vast and our Actions, Words and Expressions can fill their balloons or weigh down their shackles.

Sometimes we wonder how kids get to the point where they're merely surviving when they get to us. Trauma comes in many forms and impacts people differently. Kids who've been through trauma can feel foggy, unfocused and sad leaving little room for academics feeling vital to their lives. Students who live through physical, emotional and sexual abuse, fires, earthquakes, tornadoes, bullying, or loss of a family member are just a few reasons why "Those Kids" aren't always available to learn. Together, we've been experiencing a historic pandemic that has some kids, administrators, teachers and parents worried, concerned and scared. The unsettling feeling can produce behavior that appears to be defiant, but in reality when we feel scared and unsure, some tend to lash out. Give yourself grace. Give your students grace. Give each other grace.

The power educators have to empower students has no ceiling. Our kids are searching to matter and stand out in a social media world driven by standards, looks, money, and unrealistic expectations. The goal is not to fix kids. Instead we have to guide them with love, understanding & feedback. Perhaps if we stopped trying to find perfection by fixing kids in our imperfect world, and realize that our true mission is to build self-esteem and confidence, we would gain so much in allowing them to grow as the unique individuals they are. Our feedback matters.

*Strive for continuous improvement, instead of perfection.*
- Kim Collins

# Feedback with Feeling take-aways

- Feedback with feeling. Do they feel it?

- Does your feedback help kids soar, or add weight to their shackles?

- There are kids in our schools there to learn and those who show up attempting to survive.

- Knowing our kids stories helps us understand how they perceive our feedback.

- You are in control of your Actions, Words & Expressions (AWE).

# $\mathcal{G}$olden $\mathcal{G}$reeting

Golden Greetings are opportunities to connect with our students outside of teaching in the classroom. Golden Greetings are in our eyes, our tone & our smile. They establish and grow relationships with our students because our interactions are intentional.

**Student Arrival**

It is important to be physically visible when kids arrive at school or class. Stand outside the bus loop saying good morning. Give hugs, high fives, handshakes, big smiles or post pandemic, perhaps elbow bumps. All adults should be in the hallway during passing periods to avoid issues. This allows us to greet the students walking in and helps monitor hallway activity at the same time. Being proactive in our work benefits everyone because if we can avoid behavior issues or drama, by all means it will save us a lot of time.

**Unstructured Areas**

Unstructured places like hallways, lunchrooms and recess are prime locations for bullying and other undesired behaviors. Being in the hallway during passing time is an awesome opportunity to make small talk, congratulate kids, monitor behavior, and problem solve. Being present can provide clues to what's going on with students and provide opportunity to calm a spark before it turns into a roaring bonfire.

**Participate at Recess**

Yes! Once in a while play a game, shoot some hoops or jump rope with the kids. As a teacher & principal, I would get out to the playground as much as I could. The best recess memory was "March Madness." The junior high kids loved the old school game of four square and I played with them a lot. Each month we held "March Madness" and had a four square tournament. All adults and junior high kids could enter the tournament. We created brackets on posters and played out the madness each month. Janitors, paraprofessionals & teachers participated regularly and we had our superintendent play as a guest one month. It was awesome! Spending time with kids outside of time that is required in the classroom can relieve a little stress and certainly build relationships.

*Students don't care how much you know until they know how much you care.*

-Anonymous

## Golden Greetings take-aways

- It's in your eyes, your tone and your smile.

- Connect with your kids outside of the classroom. A smile. A word. A high-five.

- Be present when kids are in the hallways as much as possible.

- Our kids want to feel they matter. Your Golden Greetings will help them understand whether or not they matter to you.

- You are in control of your Actions, Words & Expressions (AWE).

# $\mathcal{H}$exagon of $\mathcal{H}$ope

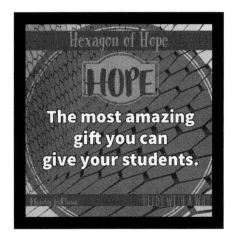

Children impacted by trauma need help seeing light at the end of the tunnel. We can help kids and families cope, heal, trust and find hope through our Actions, Words and Expressions. I created a document called the Hexagon of Hope to share with my son's teachers because on our journey there was so much I needed teachers to know. The following six phrases were my way of communicating with my son's teachers during our most difficult times. Kids who are traumatized and misunderstood need all educators to understand these six phrases because they describe the basics of what trauma can do to the brain.

**I may be scared by things that you never have to worry about. Please be patient with me.**
Soon after my son spilled his emotions, paranoia overtook him. He was certain his little brother was going to get hit by a car or someone was going to break into our home. If the sky turned dark, it

was the end of the world. He would cry, scream, hide and had frequent panic attacks. When a person loses trust in the world, vulnerability becomes lost. Please stay calm and be patient with "Those Kids." Focus on progress over perfection and realize that behavior is communication.

**I don't trust right now. Please smile at me, praise me & keep trying to get to know me.**

When you are traumatized or feel misunderstood, trust has to be rebuilt and it takes a great deal of time. All I wanted and needed was for the teachers to listen to our pain & understand my son's story. Many of our most challenging kids do not trust adults. This will be magnified more than ever in a post pandemic world and a world still trying to realize right from wrong. We are living through an extremely difficult time. We must prepare our heads & hearts for a backlash/lack of trust unlike any we've ever experienced when school returns. While at home learning with technology & packets, many places in our country burned. People were emotionally overwhelmed, hurting with pain so deep and raw it's difficult for so many of us to truly understand. The uncertainty our kids have experienced must be met with love, empathy, understanding and trust. They must trust that we are here to listen and do all that we can to understand, guide and help them on their journeys. Perhaps this will be the turning point in education where we honor Compassion before Curriculum, Relationships before Rigor and Practice Perspective like never before.

When a person's heart is racing because surroundings are uncertain, attitude regarding school work appears poor. As educators we can take behavior personally, or we can stay personally connected.

Is HE having a hard time or is he giving ME a hard time? We differentiate expectations for reading, math and science. We must do the same for behavior and motivation now more than ever before.

**I get really overwhelmed and may put my head down. Please tell me you see I'm having a hard time & tell me to take a break.**

A universal sign of struggle, exhaustion, frustration or pain is a head down. Any place other than a classroom, if we see a person with their head down, we realize something must be wrong. When kids put their heads down in class, they are communicating something. Ask how you can help. Acknowledge the distress. Acknowledge the pain. Acknowledge the resentment. Look in the mirror and ask yourself if you are offering hope or you are adding weight to their shackles. Kids struggling to survive are sometimes not available for academics. The more you can build your relationship, the more you will get out of that child, but it may not be what you get from kids ready to learn. This is a difficult concept because we live in an instant gratification world. Trauma causes emotional reactions and behaviors that take a long time to overcome.

**At times, school is the last thing on my mind because of flashbacks and I just can't concentrate. Please know I'm not trying to be disrespectful when I don't do your work.**

I have watched my son become so sad and depressed that survival was our only focus. Depression is an emotional roller coaster. Life can be ok one day and horrible the next. We have to work so hard to see each student for who they are and what they need to be successful. If we take personally the fact that some kids can't get work done on time or don't do it at all, we have failed them. Never be afraid to push back a due date or excuse an assignment. In the months and years after the spring of 2020, we must collectively realize that so many more of our kids will return to school traumatized. Our one-size-fits-all policies won't be effective, especially for "Those Kids."

**I need constant reassurance. I know it may get old, but this is what I need to get through the day. Tell me it's ok, write to me, have lunch with me and repeat often.**

My son continues to need daily reassurance. Depression and PTSD have robbed his self-esteem. The life-long work it takes to rebuild is relentless, difficult and frustrating. "Those Kids" may seem annoying or needy and perhaps sometimes they are. Our world will always have "Those Kids." Taking a few extra seconds to reassure their efforts and livelihood make a difference. Focus on Actions, Words and Expressions. They matter. A lot.

**Sometimes it's all too much and I cry, scream or act out. Please keep telling me you believe in me and do not punish me. My behavior shows my pain.**

We can't punish trauma. My son used to lose control and cry when overwhelmed. Some saw that as defiance or acting like a brat. As he gets older, he uses strong words to describe his feelings and then later regrets what he said. To an outsider, this can look like defiance, but it's not. It's a deficiency in self-control of emotions that we work on every day. I emphasize that our son has two educated parents who love and support him. We have kids in our schools who are feeling despair & distress and do not have support. I shared earlier that seeing your child in pain feels like constant electrocution. Everything is hard. Making friends, trusting teachers, doing school work, branching out to new activities or clubs, finding motivation to get up some days are all a part of what we work through every single day. He is not giving you a hard time. He is having a hard time.

I repurposed the Hexagon of Hope when consulting to help kids find their voice and adults find understanding and awareness of differing needs. We start with a picture of the child in the center hexagon with six boxes shooting out from the center. The goal of each box is as follows:

- Box 1: Me

- Box 2: I struggle with?

- Box 3: When I feel unavailable, please...

- Box 4: What I want others to know about me...

- Box 5: When you talk with me, please...

- Box 6: I'm interested in...

As a team, including the child, we fill out this hexagon together. This tool has been an excellent addition to many student plans. When we know a little more about a child's story, it gives us a better opportunity to help the child find success. Success looks different for everyone.

I dwell in possibility.

-Emily Dickenson

The Hexagon of Help full page resource & example template are featured in the Those Kids Study Guide which is available as an instant download on my website. Visit www.heidylafleur.com or scan here:

Hexagon of Hope take-aways

- Hope. The most amazing gift you can give your students.

- Kids who are traumatized and feel misunderstood need hope above all else.

- Providing hope is a lifeline for many of our kids.

- Focus on progress over perfection and realize that behavior is communication.

- You are in control of your Actions, Words & Expressions (AWE).

# *I*nterest before *I*nstruction

Knowing our students inside and out can help alleviate behavior issues in the classroom. When we put a story with every kid we teach, they become so much more than students in our schools. They are not robots. They are human beings with beating hearts, working brains and feeling souls who come from a variety of home environments. Getting to know our kids outside of instructional minutes can be the most powerful time we spend with them. When they know we're interested in them, they are ours!

Kids who come to us ready to learn are eager to share their stories with us. They want to please us and usually know how. Those who come to us struggling to survive show their stories through their behavior and although they want to please us, they usually don't know how. Any attention is better than no attention at all. With "Those Kids" we have to be creative in showing our interest because oftentimes they misperceive the intentions of teachers &

peers. Spending time one-on-one allows our true intentions to be accepted from the child's point of view. One-on-one time can be done a minute here and a minute there. The minutes add up and the connection grows. The students begin to see that we're interested in them, not just their school work. The extra minutes do not have to be spent on every child you teach. Educators are amazing, but that's a bit crazy. Many of our students get enough attention just being in our classes and interacting with us. When I talk about spending extra minutes, I'm talking about the kids who need to feel connected most, "Those Kids." When was the last time you spent time with a student outside of instructional minutes? Again, they are some of the most powerful minutes you can spend with "Those Kids." Here are some ideas for you to get the one-on-one minutes to add up:

**Lunch Groups**
Anytime you can grab lunch with a student or a group of students, it is special time outside of instructional minutes. You can talk about a variety of things and get to know about their lives. What games do they play? What teams do they like? What instruments do they play? What makes them happy or angry or grumpy? We can still accomplish minutes during the pandemic because we all have to eat! If we have to sit six feet apart, so be it. We're still connecting and that's the most important part.

**Cafeteria Visits**
After you eat, take a stroll through the cafeteria just because...because you want to say hello to your students and make sure they know they matter to you. You don't have to stay long, but the minutes add up when they see you outside of the classroom. If you are

teaching exclusively online, perhaps inviting a few kids each week to "stay for lunch" over the virtual experience would be a great opportunity to connect.

### Recess Walkthrough

Get out and get some exercise by walking through the playground, field or gym during recess. Join in a quick basketball game, jump rope session or just hang out for a few minutes. Again, I know you're busy, but never too busy to help kids know they matter which pays dividends in the classroom.

### After School Activity

Check out your students' participation in sports, the arts, choir or theater. Go to a game, a play or a concert and be sure they know you're there. Even when you can't make it, be aware of what they do and what their interests are. Open class with announcements from activities the night before and celebrate their accomplishments!

### Personal Notes

Taking a minute to write a personal note is something we can't forget in our technology-driven world. The power of a few words on a piece of paper will not soon be forgotten. As the saying goes, people who feel appreciated will do more than expected. That is the truth. Validation is critical to self-esteem.

### Interest Inventory

We get lots of academic data on kids. How about data on them as human beings? Providing an interest inventory a few times per year helps us to get to know them and allows them to share about their lives outside of academics. Be creative with what you want to know about them. Here are a few examples:

- Tell me what school is like for you.

- How can I make this year the best for you?

- If you could go anywhere in the world, where would it be?

- What makes a great teacher?

- Does anything bother you in school?

As a principal, I loved being in classrooms with kids. I would sit with them, discuss and learn with them. I would always ask when they were going to take their next test and ask if I could take it as well. They thought this was crazy cool! I would show up for the test and take it with the students. After, I would send invitations to all kids to have lunch with me in two separate groups. Those who met or beat my score were the first group. We would have lunch together and they would tutor me on the questions I got incorrect. The next day lunch was with the group who scored lower than me. As we ate, I got the opportunity to teach them some of the problems they got wrong. Interest before Instruction always.

*No significant learning can occur without a significant relationship.*
*-James Comer*

# Interest before Instruction take-aways

- When you know me, you know what I need.

- Imagine the power of spending the first week of school building community instead of rushing into instruction.

- Work to be able to give a one-minute speech on every kid you teach that has nothing to do with academics.

- If they know we're interested in them, they are ours!

- You are in control of your Actions, Words & Expressions (AWE).

# *J*ourney without *J*udgement

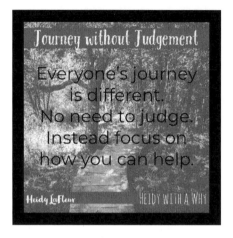

Journey without Judgement

Everyone's journey is different. No need to judge. Instead focus on how you can help.

Heidy LaFleur          HEIDY WITH A WHY

I have been a part of many IEP meetings and seen them from different lenses. I've sat at the table as a teacher, assistant principal, principal and finally as a mother. The latter by far is the most difficult. As a mom it was easy to tell which educators were all in and which were just going through the meeting motions. Those who cared looked me in the eye, warmly smiled and celebrated my son's strengths. Their reports started with what he does well and ended with how they were going to support his deficiencies. They knew my son. Those going through the motions were cold and pushed only by paperwork, not human connection. These people didn't know my son and talked about his deficiencies. It was about his problems, not how they were going to support him.

Because I sat through the process as a mom, I decided as principal we were going to run our IEP meetings, and all parent meetings, differently. A parent wants and needs to know how their child is being taken care of. This involves understanding, empathy, connection and trusting relationships. Paperwork is important and needs to be done properly, however it should not be the focus during the meeting. We started every meeting with our laptops down and offered a genuine smile, a hug or handshake (or elbow bump in our ever changing world). We were purposeful with eye contact and genuine desire to alleviate stress from the parent. We were present. I also encouraged each member of our IEP team to reach out to the parent ahead of time. Building a relationship and getting parents to trust us best starts long before any formal meeting begins.

Next, we would open the meeting by welcoming the parent/guardian and thanking them for coming. We asked parents to tell us how life was going with their child and brag about him/her. Bragging about a child you love can alleviate stress and anxiety. It makes the parent feel good about themselves and puts them at ease. In reality, when we offer parents/guardians the opportunity to brag, we have to be prepared for any kind of response. Once, when asking the parent to brag a mom said, "There ain't anything good about her. What would I have to say?" Our team quickly jumped in to brag about the student. She was an extremely difficult student, but every child has strengths. When we were present in the meetings, we saw human beings and we offered the opportunity to take a difficult situation and turn it into a powerful support while building trust with a parent. When a child has been traumatized, misunderstood or takes frequent detours from what's expected, a family needs understanding, not judgement. The stress is hard on the family, too. The paperwork, mandates, and testing will bury us if we allow it. The most important thing we can do with students and families is connect and be present.

When you judge another, you do not define them. You define yourself.

-Wayne Dyer

## Journey without Judgement take-aways

- Everyone's journey is different. No need to judge. Instead focus on how you can help.

- Be present with your students and with your parents.

- Many parents walk into IEP meetings terrified. Alleviate that fear.

- Paperwork, mandates, and testing will bury us if we allow it. Don't allow it.

- You are in control of your Actions, Words & Expressions (AWE).

# 𝒦indness for every 𝒦id

After graduating from Drake University, I moved to Chicago with my fiancé and began searching for a teaching job. Not having a clue what I was doing, I opened the Chicago Tribune (yes, the actual newspaper) and began looking. There was an opportunity with the Chicago Public Schools and I interviewed for the position and got it! The first week of school, my principal came to my classroom and questioned something I had on the wall. It read, "How are you smart?" He asked if the sign should read, "How smart are you?" and I said no. My goal was to figure out *how* my students were smart & celebrate them. I knew that kids were not robots and they all learn so differently. Finding their strengths and building confidence was what I loved most. Every child has strengths and should be celebrated. Let me be clear by sharing that I'm not talking about handing out participation trophies, instead I'm talking about celebrating unique human beings.

We can always find something positive in a student if we look hard enough.

Sometimes, we feel stressed and worried about interacting with students who take frequent detours from what's expected. Sometimes we don't feel equipped with tools to figure out how they're smart because their behaviors may interfere. Here are some tools for you:

**Genuine Words** (Always done privately, with a smile and below the student's eye level)
- I missed you! I'm really glad you're back.
- It's ok that you're late, I'm just glad you're here. Let me show you where we are.
- I need a helper in today's lesson, would you help me?
- Would it be ok if I visited you at lunch today?
- I appreciate your honesty.
- Would you rather sit in the front or the back of the room?
- Tell me what overwhelms you.
- Thanks for getting started.
- You don't have to carry all of those worries. I can carry some for you.

## Celebrating all Kids
I carried this same mentality to administration. How could we honor the kids who excelled in the classroom but also find ways to honor kids with other talents? As a school leadership team, we decided to implement Student of the Week throughout the entire school. The goal was to highlight every kid in the school by the end of the year. Each teacher nominated one student from their

class each week and wrote a simple sentence on a provided card honoring a strength. Some cards honored academics, others manners, some kindness, some athletics and others art. The purpose was to help every child feel they mattered and that we celebrated more than academic success. The cards were put on the huge bulletin board in the main school hallway with a picture of each student. I had lunch with the weekly nominees and after lunch we went to the bulletin board to read their cards. As I read aloud what each teacher said about each student, they smiled ear to ear. Spreading seeds of kindness is essential for social emotional growth.

Be a rainbow in someone else's cloud.

-Dr. Maya Angelou

# Kindness for every Kid take-aways

- Our job is to make every day the best day for every child.

- Think "How are you smart?" instead of "How smart are you?"

- Every child has strengths. As educators, we get the opportunity to help kids soar.

- All kids learn differently and one-size-fits-all teaching adds weight to kids shackles.

- You are in control of your Actions, Words & Expressions (AWE).

# si*L*ent *L*istening

Silent and listen have the same letters. It is impossible to listen if we are not silent. Many kids communicate without words. They use eye contact, shoulder shrugs and head nods. They hide under a table, and refuse to look at us. This is their way of saying something is wrong. For students who shut down and refuse to talk, try nonverbal communication because their silence may be a way to scream for help. Here is an example:

After a lesson on writing a complete sentence, Sally puts her head down on her desk. This is a pattern the teacher notices after every writing lesson. The teacher assigns work and most kids begin working. The teacher approaches Sally and privately says, "Sally, what's wrong?" No response. The teacher kindly tries again, "Are you sick?" Still no response. The teacher feels frustrated because she wants to help Sally and Sally feels frustrated because she does not want to do the work. Sally wants to be understood. She feels insecure in her writing abilities. The teacher tries a strategy called silent listening. She kneels on the floor face to face with Sally and puts her hands out, palms up. The teacher says, "I want to help you Sally. Do you like writing? Yes (shows right palm) or No (shows left palm)." Sally looks at the left palm which tells the teacher her answer is no. The teacher asks another question. "Do you think you're a good writer? Yes (shows right palm) or No (shows left palm)." Sally points to the left palm telling the teacher silently that her answer is no. The teacher then whispers to Sally, "I believe you are an excellent writer. I have one more question for you." The teacher then states, "What color do you like best? Red (shows right palm) or blue (shows left palm)." Sally touches the teacher's right palm. The teacher goes to her desk and grabs a red pen and tells Sally she can do her work using a red pen today.

This approach helps the teacher understand more about Sally's shut down & opens communication between the teacher and student. It also gives Sally a feeling of power and control over something she struggles with. Kids who avoid communicating verbally are still communicating. We have to continue to get creative in our ways to help "Those Kids" because "Those Kids" are OUR Kids!

Most people do not listen with the intent to understand; they listen with the intent to reply.

-Stephen R. Covey

# siLent Listening take-aways

- Do you hear me?

- Kids who are traumatized and misunderstood often revert to hiding, putting their heads down and silence. They are communicating with us.

- Task refusal stems from underlying fear, worry or displeasure. Search for the why.

- Kids who refuse to talk are searching for someone to truly listen.

- You are in control of your Actions, Words & Expressions (AWE).

# Meaningful Mission

How many times have you heard it? Teachers have it easy. Nights off. Weekends off. Holidays off. Summers off. That's funny. The reality is, nights are spent planning for the next day. Weekends are spent on paperwork, grading and communicating with parents. Holidays are spent getting caught up, and much of the summer is spent getting ready for the upcoming year. Finding balance as an educator takes thought, planning, commitment and execution. Taking care of yourself and your colleagues has to be a top priority and the only one who can make it a top priority is you!

Part of taking care of yourself is working on a solid foundation of self. When you know who you are, you set boundaries and practice what it takes to stay mentally strong. Your core beliefs, for example state who you are so when you feel like you're stressed and getting off track, you can revisit them. When I was an assistant principal in Chicago, we were asked to write down our core values. At the time, I thought it was silly and didn't understand the purpose. Turns out, it was one of the most powerful things I've ever done. When you know who you are, it's easier to get back up when you fall. You will fall. We all do. Know your core values so you can get back up! I'd like to share mine:

- Honesty - Even when it's difficult - it will help others grow

- Compassion - Walk in other people's shoes before making decisions and never get taken advantage of - make sure your kindness isn't mistaken for weakness

- Work Ethic - high expectations for self and others - model with words and actions

- Communicate - people who don't know can only assume - be consistent and to the point

- Appreciate - recognize greatness - appreciate it - celebrate it

- All kids can learn - regardless of what life has dealt - make it better for every child - help others understand this

- Humor - laugh - motivate - keep it real

- Grace - give it to self and others - failure is part of the process

- Never forget where I came from - teacher first, always

The other foundational piece of taking care of yourself is knowing your why. Why do you do this work? Teaching and learning are extremely difficult when done effectively. The beginning of each year we enter the honeymoon phase. Kids are on their best behavior and we aren't bogged down and overwhelmed. Come November, kids are feuding, not turning in work, talking back and our nerves are getting frayed. We are thinking, "How many days until winter break?" Winter break comes and we try to relax, but can't seem to stop thinking about all we have to do at school. We go back in January, then February and oh Lord when is spring break? We hit the April avalanche when things seem to be falling apart and we head up the May mountain wondering how we will make it. Somehow, someway, we always do! Knowing why you get up each day and do what you do builds a solid foundation assisting you when the going gets tough. Teaching is awesome in so many ways and it is certainly challenging! Know your why and post it where you can visit it frequently. My why has two parts: A visual and a quote.

<u>MY WHY</u>

**I hope my achievements in life shall be these...that I will have fought for what was right and fair, that I will have risked for that which**

**mattered, that I will have given help to those who were in need...that I will have left the earth a better place for what I've done and who I've been.**

-C. Hoppe

Pouring our heart and soul into other people's children takes relentless energy and dedication. Knowing your core values and understanding why you do what you do can help with making your mission meaningful. Take care of yourself. Take care of each other.

There are millions of cheap seats in the world today. Filled with people who never once step foot in the arena. Who will never once put themselves out there but will make it a full time job to hurl criticism & judgement & really hateful things toward us. And we have to get out of the habit of catching them. And dissecting them & holding them close to our hearts. We gotta let them drop on the floor. Don't grab that hurtful stuff from the cheap seats. Just let it fall to the ground. You don't have to stomp it & kick it. You just have to step over it and keep going.

-Brené Brown

## Meaningful Mission take-aways

- Be a community. Take care of each other.

- Never underestimate the difference you make.

- Be the best you can be in front of your students then go home and be the best you can be there. The quality of the time is more important than the quantity.

- It's ok to pause. Please do. Often.

- You are in control of your Actions, Words & Expressions (AWE).

# $\mathcal{N}$evertheless $\mathcal{N}$egotiate

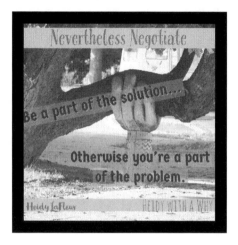

Kids who struggle with behavior are often feared by educators. Feeling powerless leads to anger and resentment for both adults and students. We can fear "Those Kids" or we can grow to understand and negotiate situations with "Those Kids." As we know, relationships with our students are built in hallways, lunchroom conversations, though inspirational notes, outside of class activities, understanding, compassion and kindness. We get to decide what we do with unexpected behavior, but we need some parameters. The goal is to keep students in our classes, if at all possible because kids who struggle with behavior are accustomed to people giving up on them.

She's not listening. He won't do what I say. They refuse to get to work. You are in control of this with your Actions, Words and Expressions. You get to decide - is he having a hard time or is he giving me a hard time? Check your tone, your expressions, your mood, and the student's mood. What is the trigger to the behavior? Remember, students who've been traumatized, are misunderstood and those who practice frequent detours from what's expected often misinterpret the intentions of others and feel threatened.

So how do we know when to ask for help when we feel a student's behavior is not negotiable? Here are some guidelines to discuss with your colleagues:

**Student is NOT unsafe to self or others**
This means:

- Student is refusing to do work

- Student has head down or hood up

- Student may say things that seem defiant when actually they're usually deficient in the appropriate communication skills when dysregulated

- Student is pacing in the room

- Student is hiding calmly under a desk

- Student won't talk

What can I say to the student? (Privately)
- It looks like you're having a hard time.

- I'm here to help you.

- I want to help you.

- Can you help me understand what you're feeling?

- Would you like to draw what you're thinking?

Remember, kids who are surviving may not be available for academics at times and that's ok. Supporting them with connection and a positive AWE will build a relationship to help the child soar.

**Student is unsafe to self or others**

This means:
- Student is throwing objects at others or in the direction of others

- Student is physically hurting himself or others

- Student's behavior is a gross and continuous disruption of classroom instruction

What can I say to the student? (As privately as safety allows)
- Your actions are not safe and I want to help you.

- I can see you're upset. This is not a safe way to work through your anger.

- Please let me help you.

If the student does not respond to your words, outside help may be necessary to keep students and staff safe. Safety is always the main priority.

Negotiating with kids, when it's safe, is a means to a positive and peaceful end. Negotiating, like bartering, can teach compromise, teamwork, self-control, self-esteem and honoring others' opinions. Nothing trumps the needs of a child. Nevertheless Negotiate.

*The most important trip you take in life is meeting people half way.*

-Henry Boyle

The Nevertheless Negotiate full page resource called Do They Stay or Do They Go? is featured in the Those Kids Study Guide which is available as an instant download on my website.
Visit www.heidylafleur.com or scan here:

### Nevertheless Negotiate take-aways

- Be a part of the solution. Otherwise you are part of the problem.

- "Those Kids" are accustomed to others giving up on them.

- You get to decide - is he having a hard time or is he giving me a hard time?

- Safety is always the main priority.

- You are in control of your Actions, Words & Expressions (AWE).

# $O$pen to $O$pposition

Teaching involves working with kids from differing backgrounds and circumstances. In a perfect school (non-existent) all administrators, teachers and staff are on the same page believing in all students. Good administrators try hard to get everyone on the same page and usually realize changing individual people's behavior is impossible. The goal is to model. Same goes for our students.

There is no secret potion when it comes to working with oppositional behavior. There is however, a magic that exists if we want to see it. If a teacher calls the social worker, counselor, principal or occupational therapist to her room, that person usually takes care of the student. Sometimes those getting called in, get called in so often they become frustrated because some teachers want them to take care of the behavior. Instead of having one person take care of the behavior, work together as a team. Great educators discuss strategies to mediate oppositional behaviors and are not afraid to learn from mistakes. They support each other because working through challenging behavior is exhausting. The goal is to raise awareness that behavior change is a long process that takes patience, empathy and grace. I encourage you to discuss, practice and model specific strategies as a team.

Effective educators believe there is a reason behind every behavior. Empathetic educators believe when a student "loses control" in their presence the student trusts the providers. They stay personally connected to the student without taking personally what the student does or says. They feel "sad for" the student instead of getting "mad at" the student. They remember not to need the last word. Some kids will yell, hit, knock over tables or desks, spit, kick and mouth off. Use these moments as opportunities to guide kids. Focus on helping them through the struggle and influence behavior by silently listening, giving the student space when needed, and agreeing when they are upset.

If we wish to see it and work at it, there is magic behind working with oppositional behavior. This is an example of having a magic wand. We all have one and if we are open to growth, unafraid to make mistakes and available to work with others to learn how to best guide challenging kids we can help all kids through rough times.

*In my world there are no bad kids, just impressionable conflicted young people wrestling with emotions and impulses, trying to communicate their feelings and needs the only way they know how.*

-Janet Lansbury

## Open to Opposition take-aways

Supporting kids who are traumatized, misunderstood and those who take frequent detours from what's expected takes five things:

- M - It's not about *Me*. As educators, it's not about us. It's about kids.

- A - *Attitude* leads everything we do.

- G - *Growing* in our practice should never ever stop.

- I - *I* can't do it alone. Lean on others around you.

- C - Behavior is communication & there is always a *Cause*. Search for it.

- You are in control of your Actions, Words & Expressions (AWE).

# $\mathcal{P}$ractice $\mathcal{P}$erspective

Perspective is our personal reality. What happened in our past is the lens through which we see all other situations. What happens in our students' lives is the lens in which they view life. Practicing perspective in our schools before making decisions and taking action is key when working with tough kids.

Your perspective plays a significant role in overall interactions with students. Your AWE can trigger a student, calm a student, help a student or make a student sink deeper into a survival state leaving him unavailable to learn. There's nothing easy about working with hard to reach kids. It's really about practicing perspective for a positive outcome. Everything you say and do is a choice. Every choice has a consequence.

I grew up in an alcoholic household, therefore I have perspective on what it's like to live in an environment where screaming, stress and tension were always high. Your perspective of growing up could be completely different. The key is being able to turn the corner to see life from another angle and possess the desire to learn more about life in another person's shoes.

If you lived in a crowded apartment with roaches, that's your perspective on a home. If you lived in a four-story mansion with a butler and chef, that's how you see the world. Sometimes what messes us up is the picture in our heads of how we believe things are supposed to be. Just because things were a certain way for us, doesn't mean they were that way for others.

You may see a red rose and it reminds you of your wedding flowers. A red rose to a friend may remind her of her mother's grave. The smell of cookies to you may be memories of grandma's kitchen during the holidays, yet to another could be the smell of abuse. Do all that you can to be open to how others view the world. Curiosity helps us grow. Judgement inspires ignorance.

*When I was 5 years old, my mom always told me that happiness was the key to life. When I went to school, they asked me what I wanted to be when I grew up. I wrote down "happy". They told me I didn't understand the assignment and I told them they didn't understand life.*

-John Lennon

# Practice Perspective take-aways

- Behavior tells a story. Perspective gives it a chance to unfold.

- The way you view a flower may not be how someone else views the flower.

- Human behavior is an attempt to communicate. Our response is communication as well.

- Some kids come ready to learn. Others are barely surviving. Recognize the difference & act upon it.

- You are in control of your Actions, Words & Expressions (AWE).

# Question then Quiet

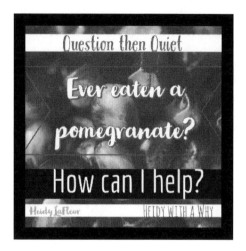

Have you ever asked anyone a question and received a strange look in return? There are constructive ways to use questions in the classroom to promote private conversations, to build relationships & finally to quiet the talker.

**Using Questions to Promote Privacy**
Power struggles happen when each participant is trying to save face. Teachers don't want to look bad in front of students and students craving power, do not want to look bad in front of peers. Kids feed off of our reaction to their misbehavior. The goal is to avoid power struggles at all costs.

Questions are powerful because they cannot be argued. They allow us to buy time between conversation and avoid defensive backlash. Promoting privacy when students act inappropriately takes away the public stage where power struggles shine. Stay calm. Refuse to take their behavior personally and know all kids communicate differently.

Kids argue and misbehave for many reasons including to seek attention, loss of power or to gain control. Kids come from many circumstances that cause them to bring resistance, sadness, anger, hostility and apathetic attitudes into our classrooms. Knowing this allows us to create an environment to ask questions regarding behavior instead of demanding expected behavior that sets the stage for a power struggle.

**Using Questions to Build Relationships - Ask then Listen**
Provide opportunities for students to talk about themselves. Asking questions says we're interested and we want to know more.

- You don't want to do 10 problems? No problem. How many is it going to take for you to show me you know how to multiply?
- Your coat is really cool. Where did you get it?
- Nice shoes. They new?
- Watch the game last night?
- Did you see the police cars on the corner this morning before school?
- How's grandma doing?
- You are so creative. Will you be joining art club?
- If you could eat anything tonight, what would it be?
- I got detention when I was a kid too. Want to hear about it?
- Do you have a favorite movie star?
- Why do you walk alone at recess?
- I noticed your hands are dirty. Can I offer you some soap?
- I have an extra school sweatshirt in the closet. Would you like to have it?
- Sweet shirt. Think I can get one in my size?
- You seem angry. Want to talk about it?
- Who gets you up in the morning?

- How is college going for your sister?
- How's mom's new job?
- Any plans this weekend?
- Can I tell you a story about my crazy son?
- Math was hard for me too. Can I share how I got through it?
- Is there something I did to upset you?

**Using Questions to Quiet the Talker**

A strategy to use when working with the student who likes to comment on everything is to ask the student an off-the-wall question privately using no sarcasm. Many of us try the "teacher look" and close proximity when trying to help a student realize their behavior is disruptive. After exhausting the look and location, try walking next to the child and asking privately, "Ever eaten a pomegranate?" or "Have you ever thought about how the blade under a lawn mower cuts the grass?" or "Can you recite the Star Spangled Banner?" The purpose for asking a question is to render the child speechless for a moment so he or she realizes their commenting is disruptive. Usually a kid will look at us like we're crazy when we ask an off-the-wall question, but it's a strategy to quiet the talker. At least for a bit.

*You can't go back and change the beginning, but you can start where you are and change the ending.*

-C.S. Lewis

- Ever eaten a pomegranate?

- Avoid power struggles at all costs. No one wins a power struggle. Think about your intention.

- Many times, kids think we're "perfect" because we are adults and educators. Share your struggles through questions too.

- Asking strange questions to bring back a talkative student can give the student the attention spotlight he may be looking for.

- You are in control of your Actions, Words & Expressions (AWE).

# Relationships before Rigor

Relationships before Rigor
Get down to their level. Look them in the eye. Ask about their night, their family, their activities...

repeat over & over & over – that's how a relationship is built.

Heidi LaFleur                    HEIDY WITH A WHY

Most general educators are trained to study curriculum, plan lessons, teach content, create projects and rubrics, offer feedback and evaluate student performance. The focus is not usually on understanding behavior, working through special needs, refocusing distracted kids, mental illness, considering trauma, emotional stress, behavioral deficiencies or strategies to cope with dysregulated children. It doesn't make a whole lot of sense, does it? Of course content, plans and curriculum are important, yet how do we teach when we aren't sure how to handle certain behaviors?

Compassion and understanding are essential to alleviating distress with "Those Kids." Relationships are the foundation for success. After serving for 20 years in schools, I've learned that some educators struggle to build relationships with kids. We watch a child with behavior challenges do awesome first period with one teacher and flounder second with someone else. Common sense asks, what is one doing, or what happens in one class, and not the other?

I often ask teachers if they see their kids. I mean really see them. Do they talk at them or with them? Do they work to know them as people and not just students? Do they apologize when they make a mistake? Do they use manners with their kids? Do they smile, love, empathize and show compassion. Do they know who's there to learn and who comes in struggling to make it through the day? Do they acknowledge kids who need a break? Do they speak privately when correcting a behavior or praising? Do they put Relationships before Rigor?

I recall one of my students, Ashley who came to school dirty every day. She had dirty fingernails and her hair was a hot mess. She did not smell pleasant. Her mom was raising three kids alone and had a problem with alcohol. I helped Ashley work through bullying and self-esteem issues. I partnered with our school nurse and bought a hair brush, hair ties, a toothbrush, toothpaste, deodorant, hand soap, a nail brush and nail clippers for Ashley. We put it all in a pink cosmetic bag, knowing pink was her favorite color. We surprised Ashley with the supplies and met her 15 minutes before school started to help her get ready. We practiced brushing her hair and tying it back nicely. Ashley brushed her teeth every morning and washed her hands. When I talk about building relationships this is what I mean. Going out of our way to help a student. Kids started asking to sit next to her. Her self-esteem improved, which led to improved connections with peers and teachers. She felt understood and therefore put more effort into her work. It is truly amazing what going the extra mile can do for a kid. Rigorous curriculum will always be important, however Relationships must come before Rigor. Always.

Kids don't learn from people they don't like.

-Rita Pierson

## Relationships before Rigor take-aways

- Get down to their level. Look them in the eye. Ask about their night, their family, their activities...repeat over & over & over - that's how a relationship is built.

- See them with not only your eyes, but with your heart and soul.

- Be open to growth from those who understand behavior. Learn from them.

- Go the extra mile. It's always worth it.

- You are in control of your Actions, Words & Expressions (AWE).

# Sorry, so Sorry

Apologizing seems simple, yet is often forgotten. The power of an apology to a student, colleague or parent builds relationships & culture. As a teacher, I asked my kids for forgiveness often. I found it comforting to be human and modeled it with my AWE. Here are a few examples:

- If the majority of my kids bombed a test, I would say, "Ok guys, looks like Mrs. LaFleur didn't do very well teaching this concept. I apologize and I will reteach it differently. Then we will retake the test because I know you are so much smarter than these scores."

- "Lauren what's bothering you? You've looked sad ever since you walked in this morning. I am so sorry to see you this way. What can I do to help?"

- "I'm sorry that I seemed so impatient this morning. I had a lot on my mind and I didn't mean to take it out on you guys."

I took the same values to administration and the most powerful story in asking for forgiveness came from my first year as a principal.

Early on I became obsessed with our new evaluation system. I read books and watched teaching videos practicing how to score and evaluate teacher performance. My goal was to provide quality feedback for teachers, while being as fair as possible. One day during an informal observation, I observed a classroom of students reading an article about bats from 1983. It was 2013. The copies of the article were tattered and some of the information obsolete. I was surprised because Mrs. T was a very good teacher in many ways. She built self-esteem, cared very much about, and challenged her students. Policy stated administrators provide written feedback using a rating system and evidence from the classroom observation. I provided Mrs. T written feedback stating the bat reading was "unsatisfactory" because the articles were tattered and the information was written 30 years prior. She wrote me an email stating that my feedback hurt her because she didn't feel she was an unsatisfactory teacher. I wasn't trying to tell her she was an unsatisfactory teacher, but that's how she perceived it. My intention was to get Mrs. T to use information from the present. Mrs. T took this feedback to mean she was an unsatisfactory teacher. I allowed policy to rule my practice and I hurt her. I should have had a conversation with her before I gave her feedback in writing. I needed to be more clear that using an article from 30 years ago was the unsatisfactory part, not her teaching of the information. What matters most is not our intentions, but how our feedback is perceived. That's why apologizing is so powerful.

I tore up the written feedback and put it in an envelope. I walked to her classroom and handed her the envelope and said I was sorry she thought my feedback came across that she was an unsatisfactory teacher. I gave her a hug and told her that I let policy get in the way of my true purpose. I was disappointed in myself for losing sight of my true leadership goals. We both grew that day, but I grew more because she forgave me.

*The first to apologize is the bravest. The first to forgive is the strongest. The first to forget is the happiest.*

-Unknown

## Sorry so Sorry take-aways

- I'm sorry. Two extremely powerful words.

- You don't have to be perfect. Your students don't have to be perfect either.

- Apologizing makes you human.

- Never be afraid to make a mistake.

- You are in control of your Actions, Words & Expressions (AWE).

# $\mathcal{T}$ell $\mathcal{T}$hem your story

We all have stories. Do your students know the reading struggles you overcame to become a successful adult? Do they know you scored poorly on standardized tests? Do they know you were a state champion? Surface level relationship building is important too. What is your favorite animal, color, food, etc. Share this as well, but never be afraid to go deeper. In all we do and say, please remember someone has trusted their child to you. Be sure your AWE helps their balloons soar and doesn't add weight to their shackles.

In order to be our best self, we can use the following strategies to reflect on our own actions and behaviors. This activity can be a great tool to revisit yourself and prepare to share yourself with your students. Human connection is extremely powerful and together we learn that we are never alone in life. Someone may be having similar experiences as we are and confiding in each other helps us feel relieved. As Ian Maclaren said, "Be kind, for everyone you meet is fighting a hard battle."

This activity allows you to write out those who've influenced you, write out your core values, your pet peeves, and ultimately your why. Take the time to reflect on this. You deserve it.

Name at least three people who either positively or negatively impacted you during the following times. These people helped shape the person you are today.

## WHO ARE YOU? WHAT IS YOUR WHY?

Know yourself so you can give your best to others.

| Name | Elementary Years | Name | High School Years |
|------|------------------|------|-------------------|
|  | +  - |  | +  - |
|  | +  - |  | +  - |
|  | +  - |  | +  - |

| Name | College | Name | Career |
|------|---------|------|--------|
|  | +  - |  | +  - |
|  | +  - |  | +  - |
|  | +  - |  | +  - |

What are your core values? Your core values will lead your Actions, Words & Expressions with your students.

## My Core Values

| Core Value | Description |
|------------|-------------|
|  |  |
|  |  |
|  |  |

What makes you craziest about kids? Identify it. Work on it. Be proactive instead of reactive. What is your why? Why do you work with kids every day?

What makes me Crazy?

My Why

$T$ell $T$hem your story

Tell them your story. Your story is made of stepping stones that can help your students on their journeys. Let them see you as a human being who makes mistakes, fails & recovers. Be vulnerable. Be real. Be you.

Tell the story of the mountain you climbed. Your words could be a page in someone else's survival guide.

-Morgan Harper Nichols

The Tell Them your story full page template is featured in the Those Kids Study Guide which is available as an instant download on my website.
Visit www.heidylafleur.com or scan here:

### Tell Them your story take-aways

- Human connection begins with sharing your story.

- Revisit your core values and your why often.

- When you know yourself well, you can get through anything.

- Each day, your AWE helps write a child's story.

- You are in control of your Actions, Words & Expressions (AWE).

# 𝒰nderstand and 𝒰plift

What do we carry in our emotional backpacks? As educators, we carry a lot with us simply because we are human beings and teaching is a significant responsibility. When we think about all that we carry, it impacts what we do and say every day. Same goes for our kids and their emotional backpacks.

When I first started teaching, I had a student, Steven, who touched everything. Every book, every desk, every person, every locker, every wall. He also picked his nose, his ears and picked at his hand until it bled and I couldn't figure out what his deal was. Our OT spent a lot of time with him and I asked her why he touched everything and was always picking at his skin. I said, "What's wrong with him?" Her response forever changed my view on kids who experience life in need of sensory input.

"He needs sensory input," she said. "Huh? What is that?" I replied. She explained to me that his body craves input of our senses and that's why he touches so much. I realized there was nothing wrong with Steven, he just experienced the world differently than I did. It was my job to learn as much as I could from the OT so I could support Steven in feeling successful.

Often kids who carry sensory needs in their backpacks are punished because they can't sit still, touch too many things, are out of their seats, chew on shirts and pencils, rock in their chairs, etc. I share this with you because when we work with a team of people who've been trained in different things, we can put together a comprehensive plan using all of our strengths. As an education student in college, I learned about teaching reading and math. I learned a tiny bit about classroom management. I learned how to write 10-page lesson plans (Ugh). I didn't learn enough about human behavior. As a teacher, I leaned on my OT, PT, speech pathologist and special education experts to understand more about behavior. If I wanted to teach academics, I had to know how to give kids the input needed to feel successful. Over the years, thanks to learning from amazing providers, I implemented many ways to help kids in need of input feel calm and ready to learn. This is the key to Understanding & Uplifting our students. Here are a few examples:

**TOOLS, NOT TOYS**
A student carrying oral sensory input needs in her backpack could use a piece of gum. Sometimes we avoid gum and mints because we think kids will put the gum in a place it doesn't belong. Acceptable use of gum and mints, used for sensory input, can be taught. I

always say this is a tool, not a toy. As you know, if you give a kid a piece of gum, she may blow bubbles, crack it and play with it. The key is not to expect the child to use it appropriately unless we teach it. If it helps a child find peace, why wouldn't we teach him/her how to use it as a tool for success?

A kid with a lot of energy in his backpack needs a plan to wear off some of that energy so he can be peaceful with himself & ultimately work successfully in school. It's ok for a child to stand and work, sit and work or move and work. Kids who need to move are going to move regardless, so being as proactive as possible will help all involved. School starts at 9:00 AM and by 9:20 AM, Ryan is all over the room. Ryan needs to move. In some classrooms we might hear, "Ryan, sit down. Ryan go to your seat. Ryan, can you read me rule #6 on our class chart? Ryan if you don't find your seat you are staying in for recess." Ryan could use a special job at 9:15 AM every day! If we teach Ryan a special job, he gets to move and we get some work out of him. Some of our kids will need jobs several times a day in order to feel success. One job could be taking a bin of books to the office each morning at 9:15 AM. This is not something we just tell Ryan to do. We show him how to do it. Ryan's job could be to load reams of paper onto a shelf, because the heavy work stimulates his need for input. Later, he can remove the reams of paper. We could fill a backpack with books and have Ryan walk to another teacher's room with a message. Again, we don't just send Ryan off into the wild, we plan his job and teach him how to do it. He gets the input he needs and we help him become available for some work. It's a win-win!

Thinking of your child as behaving badly disposes you to think of punishment. Thinking of your child as struggling to handle something difficult encourages you to help them through their distress.

-Unknown

# Understand and Uplift take-aways

- I carry more than books in my backpack. Please remember that.

- Know that we all have emotional backpacks and they impact how we use the tools in our physical backpacks.

- What if we learn to be aware of student needs instead of just expecting certain behavior.

- If you tell a fish to climb a tree...how can you help the fish find success?

- You are in control of your Actions, Words & Expressions (AWE).

# $\mathcal{V}$alue $\mathcal{V}$ulnerability

Vulnerability. As humans, being vulnerable can be frightening, especially for "Those Kids." Being vulnerable means feeling exposed or "out there" to be attacked either emotionally or physically. Who would dare be vulnerable? I believe we can give people the gift of space, time and hope to be vulnerable. Simply stated, when we can let go and be vulnerable, someone helps us carry the weight.

I thought that as I got older, life would get easier. What I've learned is that all of us deal with life in different ways. Adversity carries no bias and can hit us as individuals, as a family, as a team, as a country or as a world. As educators, the most significant impact we can leave on our kids is that we allowed them to be vulnerable with us and that starts with empathy. Notice this has nothing to do with academics, because although academics are important, they will not be able to get through to kids who have their guards up. Together, let's help our kids and colleagues let their guards down, feel accepted, love themselves and live an awesome life.

Showing empathy is actually crawling into the dark hole someone is in and sitting there with them. It's telling them, I'm here for you and want to support you. It's helping them find the light switch and turning it back on. It's letting the person know they're not alone and they don't have to carry the burden of stress by themselves. Empathy is doing, where sympathy is just saying. According to nursing scholar, Theresa Wiseman, there are four qualities of empathy we can work from to understand how to allow our kids to be vulnerable.

The first is perspective taking. This means seeing the world how others see it. Earlier I talked about practicing perspective because the only perspective we know is our reality. We have the opportunity as educators to make the choice to see life from another perspective. No one is perfect and that is an extremely difficult set of circumstances living in our society of money, greed and fame. Seeing things from another's perspective is essential to understanding "Those Kids." It's almost impossible to understand "Those Kids" if we close our minds to what life is like outside of our own. We can value vulnerability and set the stage to understand and listen to our kids by turning the corner and seeing life from a different point of view.

The second is staying out of judgement. That means no negative gossip. That means replacing our judgements with curiosity and questions in order to learn more. Judging others is a part of the problem. Being curious and asking questions to learn more about how we can help is a part of the solution.

The third is recognizing emotion in others which is overwhelmingly unselfish. Life is hard and opening our hearts to allow another in, takes energy, consistent effort and follow-through. Recognizing that a student is struggling and then doing what you can to alleviate their pain is extremely brave. Remember the trauma cycle and the only part you have control over is your reaction to their emotions. Be strong. Allow "Those Kids" to lose it sometimes. When we recognize their emotions, we can support them in dealing with the hurt.

Finally, the words we say matter. Communicating to our students that we see they're hurting or struggling and honoring the moment. Communicating to the child that we are there for them. This is not the time to go into how difficult your life is or share that "at least you." This is the time to listen and allow the feeling to come out and just be. Andrea Nair says, "Empathy is when a person accurately communicates that they see another's intentions and emotional state. It means watching our child's frustration and focusing on how life feels in that child's body, while putting our own anger and agenda into the background."

Valuing Vulnerability with our kids and colleagues is beautiful, courageous and selfless. All kids need us in this way, especially "Those Kids."

*Vulnerability is not winning or losing; it's having the courage to show up and be seen when we have no control over the outcome. Vulnerability is not weakness; it's our greatest measure of courage. People who wade into discomfort and vulnerability and tell the truth about their stories are the real badasses.*

-Brené Brown

# Value Vulnerability take-aways

- For when we feel safe...we open ourselves to guidance & opportunities for growth.

- Empathy is doing, while sympathy is just saying.

- Judging others gets us nowhere.

- Learn to listen without thinking of your own issues.

- You are in control of your Actions, Words & Expressions (AWE).

# $W$onder $W$hat happened

Our classrooms are filled with different academic, social, emotional and behavioral needs and it can feel quite overwhelming. We can do all we can to stick to the facts and keep our emotions in check. Instead of asking a student, "What's wrong with you?" when they make a mistake or act out, say, "Tell me what happened," & think, "I wonder what happened to this child to shape his behavior?" Behavior is communication and our AWE sends a message either supporting our kids, or condemning them. Wondering why a student is acting out is step one to being part of the solution.

One of the most successful things we can do as educators is avoid power struggles at all cost. No one wins a power struggle. Power struggles take up a great deal of instructional time if we allow it. A big part of avoiding these situations is our reaction to student behavior. Our students watch how we respond to difficult moments with students and that sets the tone for future behavioral situations.

Students misbehave for many reasons, many of which happen outside of the school building. When we think about kids who are surviving, some have no control, some have too much control, some want attention and others get too much attention. Some want to belong or look cool in front of their peers and others are just plain angry. Being aware that there is a reason behind behavior is helpful in navigating challenging behavior. As mentioned earlier, some kids come to school ready to learn and others come merely to survive. Identifying the kids who are surviving can help us be mindful that we can't take their behavior personally. Working with tough kids is frustrating and difficult. Know that the more time you take to get to know the child outside of instructional time, the more the child will feel cared about by you. When kids feel they matter, they are more likely to comply in the classroom.

Power struggles can be avoided by really reflecting on the resources taught in every letter of this book. Kids will make you upset. Ground yourself in the fact that your AWE can be a part of the problem or can be a part of the solution with all kids, especially "Those Kids."

*A power struggle collapses when you withdraw your energy from it. Power struggles become uninteresting to you when you change your intention from winning to learning about yourself.*
-Gary Zukav

# Wonder What happened take-aways

- What happened to you?

- Always remember there is a why behind all behavior.

- Identify those who are struggling to survive. Reach out to them every single day.

- Be mindful of our reaction to all student behavior. Our reaction sets the tone for managing future behavior issues.

- You are in control of your Actions, Words & Expressions (AWE).

# e𝒳tra fle𝒳ible

Being flexible comes with the commitment to not always treat everyone exactly the same way. The key here is communicating our intentions to our students and parents & following through on our word. Being fair means all kids get what they need to succeed. Being equal means everyone gets exactly the same thing. Kids who misbehave need adults who are flexible in their responses. Teaching expected behavior is a critical part of student improvement. Taking something away from a person and asking them to improve at the same time is quite impossible. Often we hear things like, "You don't know how to behave on a field trip so you are not going," or "Those kids don't know how to behave on the playground so they will be inside with me during recess." The only place to improve on a field trip is on a field trip. The only way to improve on the playground is by playing on the playground. What if we taught the expected behavior in the natural environment so our kids learn? The reality is that all kids must be taught behaviors we wish to see from them. Then, the expected behavior must be practiced over and over. In our world of instant gratification, changing behavior is far from instant.

When I became a principal, my school had detention and the same kids were in detention all of the time. Usually, the same teachers gave out detentions as well. I asked our staff to think about the purpose of detention. The majority of responses were a version of "because that's what we've always done." If we do things as we always have, we're not meeting the needs of the kids in front of us. My social worker at the time did a lot of classroom lessons using Julia Cook books, which gave me a solution to detention. Instead of having kids sit for 30 minutes, we read a book that matched their behavior deficiency. We included a discussion about the characters in the book and how there are similarities in the student's behavior. We planned and practiced what to do next time we were faced with making difficult choices. Kids identified with lessons in the books without realizing they were learning and picking up social skills that brought success. I will forever remember the Ramirez twins and their father. The twins used their hands to take care of business because that's what dad taught. Regardless of the conflict, one of the boys always hit another person. With the boys, we used the book *Soda Pop Head*, which is about a boy whose head was a 2-liter bottle of pop. When he got upset, bubbles rose quickly to his head and he popped with anger. After reading the book together, we discussed their emotions and assured them all emotions are ok. We role played possible solutions and discussed what the character did to overcome his anger. We even showed the book to Mr. Ramirez because honestly, we were trying to teach him not to use his fists as well. Making connections with kids through familiarity definitely makes a difference and helping with social skills is equally as important as learning to multiply. There is no magic potion for changing behavior and we must know to be patient, persistent and purposeful.

Not every situation needs a strict, by-the-book consequence. If we expect kids to learn expected behavior without being taught and practicing, we are kidding ourselves. Stretch your mindset and realize that just because this is how it's always been done, doesn't mean it's effective or right.

*At some point you just have to let go of what you thought should happen and live in what is happening.*
-Heather Hepler

# eXtra fleXible take-aways

- Stretch your mind and they will stretch theirs.

- Behavior modification takes time, patience, persistence and purpose.

- Allow kids to live through natural consequences by teaching them expected behavior in their natural environment.

- Understand the difference between fair and equal.

- You are in control of your Actions, Words & Expressions (AWE).

# $\mathcal{Y}$es to $\mathcal{Y}$et

The word "Yet" is one of the most powerful in our language. Adopting this influential growth mindset is contagious and necessary to sustained improvement and growth. The words "I can't" are frequent among children. We often hear, "I can't do this math," or "I can't tie my shoe," or "I can't get my serve over the net." Imagine the power of responding with a simple, "Yet." Students and children pick up the response and use it themselves. It becomes a habit in their vocabulary because of the constant repetition.

As educators we can make every school day a positive experience by utilizing a growth mindset. Our society craves instant gratification. Ordering food, requesting a ride, posting news stories and articles happen in seconds. Understanding behavior takes time, practice, patience and struggle. It's about the perspective to help and guide our kids on their journeys instead of trying to fix them. It's the power of knowing some kids are ready and some just aren't ready yet. It's a marathon, not a sprint. It's a journey, not a destination. It's life.

The expectation of perfection sets us up for failure. The expectation that every child must be at grade level, reading by age five and calculating algebraic equations by seventh grade. Not every child is ready yet. What is the rush? Teachers feel pressure. Administrators feel pressure. Parents feel pressure, and of course, kids feel pressure. This has increased dramatically during the pandemic. Many people think kids arrive by 8:30 AM, file in and sit in perfect rows with folded hands. They've been fed, are clean and their brains are ready for learning. They say yes ma'am and no sir and comply with directions, assignments and tasks. Bells ring, teachers teach and kids learn. At 3 PM, everyone leaves and nobody looks back. Yeah, right. That's not close to what happens on a daily basis.

Some teachers spend extra hours before and after school creating lessons, writing plans, correcting assignments, sharing feedback and delivering amazing content. Some understand the importance of social emotional health of our kids and some don't. Some teachers are flexible, helpful, collaborative and yearn to learn more. Some stay in their rooms, find problems for every solution and talk negatively about kids. I encourage you not to allow it, even though it's hard. Administrators, be careful allowing negative staff members to hijack meetings or staff development with whining and complaining. One of my favorite quotes by Todd Whitaker says it all, "The culture of any organization is shaped by the worst behavior the leader is willing to tolerate."

In a growth mindset, challenges are exciting rather than threatening. So rather than thinking, oh, I'm going to reveal my weaknesses, you say, wow, here's a chance to grow. No matter what your current ability is, effort is what ignites that ability and turns it into accomplishment.

-Carol Dweck

# Yes to Yet take-aways

- Yes you can...just not yet!

- Respond with an excited, "YET!" when kids share what they think they can't do.

- Life is a journey for all of us. Some of us are there, and some of us are not there YET.

- Our society craves instant gratification. "Yet" allows us to be ourselves.

- You are in control of your Actions, Words & Expressions (AWE).

# Zilch to Zero tolerance

Some schools use zero tolerance policies that mandate predetermined punishments or consequences. Most are severe, punitive and exclusionary. Our mindset matters when working with tough kids. In order to create an atmosphere where behaviorally deficient students can work to better their behaviors, we must be doing the following in every classroom and every school:

- Constantly building strong, trusting relationships.

- Providing our teachers with support & practical strategies to handle behavior

- Teaching and expecting solid classroom management.

- Truly believing that this is about kids and not about us.

- Continuously learning the why behind behavior and making every effort to alleviate distress in the life of a child.

- Providing a team of mental health advocates for our schools to help our teachers and students navigate life.

Knowing that a kid's behavior tells his story shows understanding of the behavior modification process. Behavior modification takes time, patience and belief in consequence over punishment. Consider the following behavioral mindsets when it comes to school:

**Consequence Mindset vs. Punishment Mindset**

| Consequence Mindset | Punishment Mindset |
|---|---|
| If we want to change a child's behavior, we model, teach and help students grow their coping skills for life; *we consequence*. | If we want to feel instant gratification that the child needs to pay for his/her actions; *we punish*. |

**Consequence Mindset**

Consequence Mindset involves giving consequences with calm, factual statements and composure. This means the adult tells the student privately her behavior was inappropriate, states the facts calmly with no judgement or sarcasm. The purpose is to communicate to the student that behavior must change and the consequence given aligns with changing behavior. In a consequence mindset, adults seek the why behind the behavior and realize that time owed can't be sitting in detention expecting a light to come on and a child realizes what needs to change with his/her behavior. We have to teach the behavior we want to see. Here is what consequence mindset looks like:

Ali struggles to control her temper when she is asked to do unpreferred tasks. She was asked to get her science book out and turn to page 86 to play a review game for an upcoming test. Ali slid her science book off of her desk and stated, "I hate science. I'm not doing it." The teacher picked up Ali's book, opened to page 86 and set it on Ali's desk. She continued with the lesson. Ali again slid the book off of her desk, got up and started emptying a cup of pencils onto the floor. She pulled every tissue from the box and threw those around as well. The teacher continued to teach. Ali was not a danger to self or others and the teacher wanted to keep her in class. The teacher knew Ali's parents were going through a rough divorce and thought that could be part of her behavior. The teacher also knew that Ali's behavior was inappropriate and she would need a consequence. Ali went back to her seat and did not participate in the review lesson. After class, the teacher asked Ali privately to stay after. The teacher told Ali she was sorry she felt upset in class and told her she would never go to her house and pour out her pencils. She told Ali her behavior was inappropriate and asked if she wanted to pick up the pencils or tissues first. As Ali started with the tissues, her teacher started with the pencils. Together they picked up the classroom and discussed her anger and how she would make up the review for the test. Her consequence was picking up the mess she made. With this consequence, the teacher was building a connection with her so Ali knew the teacher was not giving up on her and wanted to help her.

## Punishment Mindset

Punishment Mindset is given hastily with gritted teeth and elevated blood pressure. This means the adult is visibly upset and may speak to the child publicly. The purpose is adult satisfaction & believing the kid needs to pay for his/her actions. As human beings, we all get frustrated, annoyed and angry, but the way we practice perspective regarding students will be the tipping point for which mindset we live in our districts, schools and classrooms. Punishment Mindset seeks to inflict misery by taking away recess, kicking kids out of class and blaming administration for "not doing anything about this child." Punishment mindset is not interested in teaching behavior, it expects the behavior to change because of the punishment. Same situation. Here is what punishment mindset looks like:

Ali struggles to control her temper when she is asked to do unpreferred tasks. She was asked to get her science book out and turn to page 86 to play a review game for an upcoming test. Ali slid her science book off of her desk and stated, "I hate science. I'm not doing it." The teacher told Ali to pick up her book. Ali didn't pick up her book, got up and started emptying a cup of pencils onto the floor. She pulled every tissue from the box and threw those around as well. The teacher told Ali to go sit down. Ali didn't. The teacher yelled at Ali to get out of her classroom for being disrespectful. After class, the teacher wrote Ali up for disrespect and assigned two detentions. Her punishment was detention which gave her no guidance on how to handle her mistake or her emotions.

The key is to remember we have no control over how kids come to us, but we do have control over our actions, words and expressions. The challenge is to come together as a school community and create a mindset with actionable steps to truly change behavior. We must wonder what happened, understand intent, discuss and teach expected behavior and bring mental health professionals into our schools to support our teachers.

I'll never forget Ryan, a sweet and kind 7th grader, who always did what he was asked. At our school, we had a zero tolerance no-see, no-hear cell phone policy which meant if kids brought cell phones to school, they were not to be seen or heard in class. One day I heard a ding that sounded like it came from Ryan's pocket. I quietly & privately asked Ryan to turn off his phone. I continued teaching for many reasons. First, I could tell Ryan was mortified and making a big deal out of this was not going to behoove anyone. Second, Ryan's phone had never gone off in class and it was not a distraction to our lesson. We all make mistakes, but it doesn't mean every mistake has to be acted upon. We don't get a speeding ticket every time we speed, but unfortunately, that isn't true with zero tolerance policies.

I thought the issue was over until the assistant principal came to my classroom after lunch and asked for Ryan. I didn't think much of it until he returned to class in tears. Ryan gathered his things. I followed him into the hallway to ask what was going on and he said he was being sent home because his phone went off in class. He was upset with his mom for texting him Happy Birthday and that was the ding we heard. He said he never has his phone on in school and he forgot to turn it off. I told him I was so sorry and after that I was speechless. After talking with the assistant principal, he informed me that there is zero tolerance for cell phones and if a student's phone is heard, they will be sent home for the day. I asked if he talked to Ryan about his intent, his story or if he was aware of his excellent track record. He said it didn't matter because zero tolerance means zero tolerance.

During the same year, I had an 8th grade student, Lance come to school high almost every day. Lance admitted to being high and reeked of marijuana. The zero tolerance policy for drugs at our school was for possession, not for being high. Lance never had drugs on his person or in his locker and therefore, according to school policy, he could come to school high. When we questioned this policy we were told that we couldn't prove he was high and we were asked how we knew what marijuana smells like. So Ryan got sent home for having his cell phone ding in class, but Lance got to fly high in school because policy said so. We owe it to our kids to ask questions, challenge policies and advocate for them. They get one chance in school and we get one chance to make every day the best day for every child.

If we want to change a child's behavior, we model, teach and help students grow their coping skills for life; we conse- quence. If we want to feel instant gratification that the child needs to pay for his/her actions, we punish.

-Heidy LaFleur

The Zilch Zero tolerance full-page resource called Consequence Mindset vs. Punishment Mindset is featured in the Those Kids Study Guide which is available as an instant download on my website. Visit www.heidylafleur.com or scan here:

## Zilch Zero tolerance take-aways

- Fair is not equal. Fair is giving appropriate consequences to grow as human beings.

- It's never too late to change how you deal with kids like Ali!

- Behavior modification takes time, patience and belief in consequence over punishment.

- You can't punish trauma.

- You are in control of your Actions, Words & Expressions (AWE).

# 2020 Perspective

This book was completed during a historic & for many, a very painful time in life. The majority of the country and many parts of the globe were on lockdown because of the COVID-19 virus that turned our world inside out. Our kids were told to stay home and teachers told to teach through a screen or a packet. Parents took on the role of educator, many people lost jobs or businesses, some went hungry and others sunk into deep depression. The NBA, NCAA basketball tournament, MLB, and NHL all postponed or canceled. Kids lost access to their grandparents, schools, teachers, sports, musicals, proms, graduations, and were taught to stay "socially distant" from their friends. Award ceremonies and graduations were held online, if at all, and we were advised to wear a mask and stay six feet apart. The power of human connection took priority because we were in need of a hand to hold or someone to embrace. Time stood still. We stayed home. It was unsettling. Yet many rose to the occasion preparing school lunches for kids at home, building quality time into e-learning, going the extra mile to connect with a kid, sharing medical resources, struggling to online learn with our own kids, playing board games, going for walks...Pausing in this whirlwind society filled with greed, questionable integrity & the expectation of perfection. Perhaps the pause was necessary because our perspective on "normal" life was extremely challenged and what followed would encourage many of us to dig deeper into our purpose to change the world.

After we witnessed a virus that will be written in history books and we thought we couldn't endure more, our world took on another gut-wrenching tour questioning ethics, equality, leadership, media & justice. There were peaceful protests. There were riots. There was looting. There was anger & anguish that filled our world with more questions.

In a society that struggles to understand challenging behavior, we must advocate for the rights of all human beings above money, greed and power. Regardless of race, color, religion, sexual orientation, national origin, disability or age, we are all human beings with a heart, a soul and stories that need to be heard. We have ignored too many things for far too long and the mental health of our society must be the foundation for all else. Our kids are going to need us in different ways moving forward. Be a part of the solution or else you are a part of the problem.

### Acknowledge before Accusation
Listen to understand the intent of behavior while using non-accusatory language.

### Bonfire Behavior
Take personal accountability that our Actions, Words & Expressions affect the outcome of any situation.

### Compassion before Curriculum
Curriculum guides are a waste of words if compassion doesn't exist in our classrooms.

## Defiant vs. Deficient

Work to understand and empower our deficiencies & realize that when our stories aren't heard, many of us turn defiant.

## Empower before Ego

Be certain to include the entire team. It is a collective responsibility to raise our future.

## Feedback with Feeling

Meet people where they are and provide uplifting & encouraging feedback. Words matter.

## Golden Greeting

Use the look in your eyes, your facial expressions & your heart to greet all people and never fear to take "academic minutes" to build human connections.

## Hexagon of Hope

Hope is the greatest gift we can give our children. Be the bridge to empower all kids to be proud of who they are. Advocate for every child.

## Interest before Instruction

Aim to know our kids' stories. Build trust before expecting them to listen to our instruction.

## Journey without Judgement

Walk in others' shoes first before forming an opinion. Be curious instead of judgmental.

### Kindness for every Kid
Recognize & celebrate the strengths of EVERY child.

### siLent Listening
Listen to them. Their silence may be screaming for help.

### Meaningful Mission
Take care of yourself. Find life/work balance. Take care of each other. Pause. Vent. Reset. often!

### Nevertheless Negotiate
Know when you can negotiate a situation with a student and when the situation calls for more help. Error on the side of keeping kids in class.

### Open to Opposition
Don't let behavior come as a surprise. Every behavior has a why. Work to discover it.

### Practice Perspective
Our personal realities become our lens to life. Learn about life from many points of view. Never stop growing as a human being.

### Question then Quiet
Build relationships by asking questions. Be curious & interested in others' stories.

### Relationships before Rigor
Genuine human connection builds relationships. We have the power to change the world by listening, empathizing and loving.

## Sorry so Sorry

Realize we may be wrong & apologize for it.

## Tell Them your story

Our stories are stepping stones to the success of others. It is critical to our growth & the growth of others to share our stories.

## Understand & Uplift

Know that backpacks are filled with emotions, experiences, struggles and strengths, not just books. Give them what they need.

## Value Vulnerability

Empathy is understanding that a child is stuck in a hole. Get in the hole and provide an opportunity for the child to be heard. Learn to empathize by connecting, acknowledging emotions and allowing another to communicate.

## Wonder What happened

Let go of saying, "What's wrong with you?" and replace it with, "What happened to you?"

## eXtra fleXible

This is how we've always done it needs to go bye-bye. Expected behavior must be taught.

## Yes to Yet

Open ourselves to growth every single day. The best is YET to come.

## Zilch Zero tolerance

Every situation is different. Zero tolerance policies promote punitive mandatory punishments that do not teach appropriate behavior. Punishment mindset is about adults. Consequence mindset is about kids.

Effective teaching is hard. Working with kids who struggle with emotions is hard. If through this pandemic and civil unrest we haven't turned a corner to know that our teachers and students need mental health support in school, shame on us. Counselors, nurses and social workers should not be a luxury. They are beyond "essential" for the sake of our kids and our future.

It's time we hit the reset button. Our "normal" isn't working. We cram our most vulnerable special education kids on buses and give them paraprofessionals that are paid peanuts with no benefits. We expect teachers to do it all in a world where the partnership of mental health providers has been lacking for far too long. We expect general education teachers to understand behavior, modify work, deal with mental illness and we give them little training. We wonder why so many are burned out. We stress test scores and expect all kids to be at certain levels and if not, we've failed. That's ludicrous. All of our kids are different and have different needs. Together we must turn the focus to people over product and create a new normal that celebrates all races, colors, religions, sexual orientations, national origins, disabilities & ages. We are all human beings with beating hearts, powerful souls and stories that need to be heard. *I see you educators. I hear you, too.* **Thank you for all you do to make a difference in this world.**

The posters you see throughout *Those Kids are OUR Kids* are available for $10 as an instant download on my website. There are 31 colored, 8x8 posters in all.

Visit www.heidylafleur.com or scan here:

# Meet the Author

Heidy LaFleur is a vibrant, positive and common sense leader with explosive passion for **helping people understand trauma & the critical importance of social emotional learning**. She is a forever teacher, former school administrator and most importantly, **a mother who has lived through a life-changing trauma with her family**. As an assistant principal, the unthinkable happened in a place where she never imagined was possible. She wakes up every morning to spread the message that our job is to make EVERY day the BEST day for EVERY child.

With her personal experience being the foundation of her work with kids who struggle, she has worked with hundreds of students in need of an understanding, positive and compassionate adult in their lives. **Her true purpose in life is to help others with strategies that impact the lives of children of all ages & behaviors.** She is the founder and president of Heidy with a WHY, Inc. where she provides keynote speaking, professional development and consulting opportunities across the country.

Heidy received her Bachelor of Science in Education at Drake University where she earned a full volleyball scholarship. Her graduate work in Educational Leadership took place at Northeastern Illinois University. She has authored *Hop on the Clue Bus - A Common Sense Guide to Leadership, Hop on the Clue Bus A*

*Common Sense Guide to Conquering Teacher Evaluation* and *Those Kids are OUR Kids.* In 2016, she was awarded the Double D Award from Drake University, the highest honor bestowed on alumni student-athletes for work in their field of study. Heidy is a grateful wife of a firefighter/paramedic and proud mother of three beautiful children.

Topics include:

* Educator self-care
* Trauma-Informed Teaching
* Social Emotional Learning Strategies
* Student Behavior Strategies
* Identifying your why, focus & drive

Bring Heidy to your group in person, virtually or download the videos to watch at any time.

administrators, teachers, special education department, paraprofessionals, social workers, counselors, substitute teachers, security guards, nurses, police officers, paramedics, bus drivers, parents, pta, board of education & community members

It truly takes a village...and we all impact kids.

# Resources for Educators

This study guide compliments *Those Kids are OUR Kids* with 26 strategies to learn about and work through your current practices as an administrator, teacher, education provider and parent. It comes with a BONUS called Five practical & powerful steps to understand trauma.

Excellent for administrators, teachers, education providers, law enforcement, medical practitioners & parents. Awesome resource for teams and districts to work together on their practices.

$15 instant download

# Colored Posters

31 colored posters that serve as visual reminders of the strategies. Daily reminders help form habits and help us grow as educators and parents.

$10 instant download

# Videos

Each 60-minute video goes deeper into each of the letters. Use as a support to the book and study guide, a refresher or for continuing education hours.
Powerful. Engaging. Inspiring.

$40 each - instant download

Made in the USA
Columbia, SC
26 October 2024

45094785R00096